A Very Pleasant Evening
with Stevie Smith

Stevie Smith

A Very Pleasant Evening with Stevie Smith

Selected Short Prose

A NEW DIRECTIONS BOOK

Copyright © James MacGibbon 1937, 1938, 1942, 1950, 1957, 1962, 1966, 1971, 1972, 1981

Manufactured in the United States of America.
Published by arrangement with Farrar, Straus & Giroux.
New Directions Books are printed on acid-free paper.
First published as New Directions Paperbook 804 in 1995.

Library of Congress Cataloging-in-Publication Data:

Smith, Stevie, 1902-1971.
    [Selections   1995]
    A very pleasant evening with Stevie Smith : selected short prose /
    Stevie Smith.
        p.   cm.
      ISBN 0-8112-1295-5 :
      PR6037.M43A6 1995
      828'.91209--dc20
                                                    95-2273
                                                    CIP

New Directions Books are published for James Laughlin
by New Directions Publishing Corporation,
80 Eighth Avenue, New York, 10011

Contents

BESIDE THE SEASIDE
A Holiday with Children

It was a particularly fine day. The calm blue sea at unusually high flood washed the highest ridge of the fine shingle beach. It was a particular moment of high summer.

'In England,' said Helen, 'the hot August day is sufficiently remarkable to make an occasion.'

'One could roll off into it,' said Margaret dreamily, looking at the bulging sea.

The beach shelved steeply and the deep water lay in to shore; the water was also clear, you could see the toes of the paddlers, perched like fishing birds upon the upper shingle, knee-deep in the sea.

The two girls were in bathing dress, but Margaret's husband Henry sat in his sports shirt and flannel trousers in a deck-chair with his hat on.

'Yes, one could,' said Helen, 'but you won't, Margaret, you know you always stand up and take fifteen minutes to get right in.'

Helen now turned over and lay flat on her back looking from under her hands at the seaside people at their seaside pleasures.

'It is rather like the moral poem I wrote,' she said. 'Do you mind if I say it to you?' She looked anxiously at Henry.

'Not at all,' said Margaret.

'Oh well . . .' Henry sighed.

'Children . . .' said Helen firmly . . .

> *Children who paddle where the ocean bed shelves steeply*
> *Must take great care they do not,*
> *Paddle too deeply.*

Margaret, who was happy, took the poem with a smile, but Henry, who was never really happy, began to speak about the political situation.

'It is certain that the Russians have the atom bomb,' he said, 'otherwise they would not be pushing us so far over the Berlin business. Professor D.,' he went on (naming a once well-known Russian scientist), 'used to work with us at the Cavendish Laboratory in Rutherford's day, he went back to Russia several times, and then one day he went and did not come back. He was a most able man, no

1

doubt he is still working, they say nothing about him. . . . '

'Oh, please drop it,' said Helen; but she was not speaking to Henry, she was speaking to Hughie. Henry and Margaret Levison had two children: Hughie who was ten and Anna who was eight. Hughie was now coming along the beach from the next breakwater with a large shrimping net in his hands, and in the shrimping net was a jelly fish so large that it brimmed over the net, and all its strings hung down through the holes of the net and waved about as Hughie ran.

'Oh do drop it, Hughie,' said Helen again, 'or better still put it up at the top of the beach under the sea-wall in the full sun, where it may fry to death and quite burn out. Oh what a wicked face it has.'

'I think it looks rather beautiful,' said the gentle girl Margaret.

Well, perhaps it did, after all, look rather beautiful. It looks like a fried egg, thought Helen. The frills waved prettily around a large yellow centre, this was the yoke of the egg; it was the underneath side that seemed to have a face. Hughie had disobediently turned it upside down out of the net just beside his father's deck-chair, so now the wicked face was hidden.

'They reproduce themselves by sexual congress,' said Henry grudgingly.

Margaret and Helen lay baking in the sun, laughing silently to themselves. Henry was so brilliantly irascible and gloomy, truly he was a care-ridden person, but so simple and open, and of such a violent honesty and of such a violent love of what was beautiful and truthful, one could not help but love him.

Helen began to whisper in Margaret's ear (the two friends were both writers and had a great appreciation for each other's writing, which was quite different): 'That poem I showed you the other day, with the drawing of the man riding the old tired horse, and the old woman close behind him, is rather like Henry.'

'What poem was that?' said kind Margaret, who knew how Helen liked to say her poems aloud.

> *Behind the Knight sits hooded Care,*
> *And as he rides she speaks him fair,*
> *She lays her hand in his sable muff,*
> *Ride he never so fast he'll not cast her off.*

Margaret sighed, and turned her head away from Helen. 'That poem has rather a gothic feeling,' she said; 'it is sad too.'

At this moment Major Pole-Curtis came galloping by with his little boy David.

'Hallo, hallo, hallo,' he cried in his deep musical voice, 'not been in yet, and a lovely day like this? Slackers,' he said, 'the water is quite warm, isn't it, David?'

'So long all,' said David, who looked rather blue. 'Helen,' he cried, as his father tore off with him, 'H-e-l-e-n!'

The baby-wail of 'Helen' came back to them on the wind of their flight, and Hughie, who was squatting rather restlessly beside his mother, began to jeer.

'Helen!' he mimicked. He got up and began to prance round Helen, shouting in his shrill penetrating voice, 'David loves Helen, David loves Helen'.

The major and his family were at the same hotel as Helen and her friends, and had the next table to theirs in the dining-room. David told everybody in the hotel that he was going to marry Helen.

'Will you be quiet, Hughie,' said Henry. 'Ah, the Major,' he said, as if he had just woken up to the fact that they had been running past. There they were, now in the distance, still running.

'He was awfully cross because David and Colin were late for lunch yesterday,' said Hughie. 'Do you know he gave Colin a terrific thrashing.'

'What!' said simple Henry, as impressed and horrified as his son had meant him to be. He turned to his wife, 'I suppose that is the correct way to bring children up; you and I, Margaret, are of course quite wrong. I expect he is unfaithful to her frequently, and then he comes home and confesses "all" and says, "Muriel" (or whatever her name is), "Muriel, I have behaved like a cad." '

Henry looked pleased with himself for this flight of fancy, and especially pleased because it was so well received by the girls, with such a lot of laughter.

'I think I shall bathe now,' said Margaret.

She stepped into the sea and stood with the sea washing gently round her knees looking out to the horizon of the sea where the heat mists played tricks with the passing ships. The great liner that was passing down channel from Tilbury seemed to be swimming in the high air, because the dark band of mist that hung below her made a false sea-border.

Margaret always took a long time to get into the water, when she was at last right in she would begin to swim strongly up and down parallel with the beach in a leisurely way that was full of pleasure.

'Oh,' she said, 'I wish there was no such thing as politics and problems, how wicked people are, how beyond hope unhappy, man is the most wretched of all the animals.'

'I do not think so,' said Helen, who had rushed quickly into the water and was now swimming alongside her friend, 'I think men are splendid hopeful creatures, but they have not come very far yet.'

How beautiful the water was, warm and milky; the sun burning through the water struck hot upon their shoulders washed by the sea. Helen turned on her back to rise and fall with the swelling sea (there was quite a swell on in spite of the calmness).

'It does not look as if they would come much further,' said Margaret.

'Because of the atom bomb, you mean?'

'And a good riddance to them.'

'*Them?*' said Helen. '. . . we are also the children of our times and must live and die with them. But oh what nonsense. Have you not, Margaret, seen babies trying to destroy themselves, they feel that they will burst for all that is in them: men and women are like that.'

'And perhaps they will burst,' said Margaret.

'If they do,' said Helen, 'they will still have been the high summit of creation, both great and vile beyond dreams.'

'Well, I don't think so,' said Margaret.

'Well, I do.'

'We have been having a rather deep philosophical argument,' said Margaret, as the two wet girls flopped down beside Henry, who never bathed.

'I think I shall take my shirt off for a few minutes,' said Henry.

He peeled it off over his head and replaced his large straw hat. 'How you girls can stand so much hot sun, I do not know,' he said. 'And now look at Margaret putting all that cream on her face.' Henry sighed. 'It is no good nowadays, there used to be a natural vegetable oil in the face creams, but now what is it? nothing but petroleum oil, no good at all, in fact, harmful.'

Helen, who was slopping about in the water again at Henry's feet, her elbows on the shingle ridge to keep her steady and her body afloat in the deep water where the shingle dipped, looked up into Henry's anxious face. In his intelligence, she thought, is all his care.

The child Hughie who had run off, now came back, pushing his sister Anna in front of him. 'I think Anna has poliomylitis,' he said.

'She has a stiff neck.' (Hughie was going to be a doctor when he grew up.)

'I think my breasts are beginning to grow,' said Anna.

'Breasts,' jeered Hughie, 'at eight years old, breasts, ha ha ha!'

He turned to Henry. 'Daddy, can I have sixpence, please, for another boat ride?'

'Nothing but boat rides, ice creams, pony rides. Well,' said Henry, giving him sixpence, 'I suppose that is what you think I am here for.'

'I'll come with you,' said Helen, 'so will Anna.'

They all ran off to the *Lady Grace* which, with Mr Crask in charge, was just about to start on a trip.

'Off with you,' cried Mr Crask, chivvying the children away from the stern seat where he kept his motor. He tapped them in a friendly way upon the behind. 'Oh, beg pardon,' he said, when he had tapped Anna, 'it's a lady.'

Anna went and sat beside her brother. She was a happy, silent child, easily silenced by her clever brother, a fair, silent child, a clever child, far cleverer than Hughie, but she was his loving slave. She had a strong neat comfortable body and wore only a pair of pants. Helen loved Anna; she thought she was like a seal.

Just as they were starting off, Major Pole-Curtis came running up. 'Just in time,' he said, and popped David on board. 'Good-bye, children,' he roared as the boat shot off, 'don't be late for lunch.'

Hughie began to entertain Mr Crask with his famous imitation of a train coming into King's Cross main-line station. His bright red hair flamed in the sunshine, his thin straight body moved delicately with the movement of the boat. He stood upright on the seat and let out a wild whistle.

'What's that, Mr Crask?'

'I dunno, me boy, a whistle, eh?'

'It's a goods train going into a tunnel on an incline,' said Hughie. He gave three short barks and a groan. 'That's the trucks closing up as the engine slows down. Chug, chug, chug, it's all right now, they're gathering speed again and coming on to the flat.'

Helen smiled at Hughie and then sighed. Hughie made himself rather unpopular sometimes, he was devoured by restless energy, he must do his train noises (or whatever it was), and he must have an audience.

'That Levison boy . . .' the Major had said one day with quite a critical eye . . . he had stopped talking when Helen had come up, but there was no doubt he would like to have smacked Hughie. *Levison*, oh of course, Helen sighed again, of course the Major would feel like that . . . he had just come back from Palestine.

She looked down at the Major's little boy David who was lying alongside with a devoted air. David had pale yellow hair and great charm; he was five years old. Helen stroked his hair and, slipping her hand under his chin, turned his face up to hers. The sun-speckled face, she thought, the smiling eyes, the assured and certain eyes, the easy authority of certain charm, there is the quality of sunlight about you, of ancient sunlight in privileged circumstances.

'Daddy is going to take us to church tomorrow,' said David. 'You come too, Helen. Helen, do!'

Hughie paused in his train noises and glanced furiously across at them. What a nuisance David was, couldn't Helen *see?*

'We are going to that old church at Lymne,' went on David in a confiding tone. 'Oh, Helen, do come, do . . . *where that nice vicar is.*'

'Oh, I don't know, I don't know,' she said, stroking again the daffodil hair, 'I don't know, David . . .'

David moved closer. 'Come on, Helen, come on, do . . . *it's the best glass in the south of England.*'

Helen laughed, she knew there would be no room for her in the major's car, with mamma who liked vicars, and papa who liked church glass . . . 'I haven't got a hat.'

'Never mind,' said David, 'I never wear mine in church.'

In the evening the hotel children, marshalled by Hughie, played cricket in the field at the back of the hotel. This was a fine wide closely-mown piece of grass stretching for a distance under the hills where the old town stood. There was also the military canal and the beautiful gardens before you came to the main road. It was now seven o'clock and the sun dropping to the soft hills threw a golden light upon the cricket field and long shadows.

The grown-ups sat on the pavilion steps and watched the game. Anna, who only played with boys, was batting; she made thirteen runs.

There were a lot of other people in the field, doing different things. An old mild person stood himself in front of the children's wicket with his back turned to them; he was watching the tennis players on the other side of the wire netting.

'Would you mind moving, please,' said David firmly; he was wicket-keeper.

Some runners came charging by. Never mind, they were soon gone.

Suddenly Henry said that he would play too.

'Oh yes,' said Margaret, 'do play, Henry.'

Helen squeezed her friend's arm affectionately as Henry took his place. 'How happy you look,' she said and began to laugh softly. What an irritating girl.

'Oh, why is it,' said poor Margaret, 'why is it that there is something so sad and tense about fathers when they play with their children; it really tears at one when they take part in the sports. Why is it?'

'Yes,' said Helen, 'it is never very touching when the mothers run in the three-legged race at schools; no, it is different.'

She squeezed Margaret's arm again, 'It will be all right, you'll see.'

Margaret said, 'Henry is more locked up in being a Jew than it seems possible.'

Oh dear, thought Helen. 'Well,' she said, 'you are Jewish too, aren't you, and you do not feel locked up in it.'

'No,' said Margaret. 'But, Helen, you cannot know quite what it is like; it is a feeling of profound uncertainty, especially if you have children. There is a strong growing anti-Jewish feeling in England, and when they get a little older, will they also be in a concentration camp here in England?'

'One sometimes thinks that is what they want,' said Helen flippantly, getting rather cross, 'they behave so extremely. Well, that is rather an extreme remark of yours, is it not, about the concentration camps, eh, *here*? If there is an anti-Jewish feeling in England at the moment it is because of Palestine.' Helen paused and went on again more seriously, 'I do not hold with the theory that the Jewish people is an appeasing, accommodating people, knowing, as some say, on which side their bread is buttered, and prepared to make accommodations with conscience for their own advantage. No, I think that they are an obstinate and unreasonable people, short-sighted about their true interests, fanatical. They have not the virtues of a slave, you see, but also they have not the virtues of a wise person.'

'Do not speak like this to Henry, please, Helen,' said Margaret. 'Oh, please, do not.'

'Of course I will not,' said Helen, and was about to pursue the subject when a closer glance at Margaret's gentle face showed that to do so would be untimely and indeed fruitless.

Darling Margaret, she thought with a pang, darling darling Margaret.

Margaret liked to live in a vegetable reverie; in this world of her vegetable reverie the delicate life of the plants, and the stones, too, for that matter, and the great trees and the blades of sharp grass and the leaves that were white when they turned upon the breeze, had a delicate obstinate life of their own. Margaret thought that people were the devils of creation. She thought that they were for ever at war for ever trying to oppress the delicate life of the plants and to destroy them; but this of course fortunately they could not do.

After the cricket match Henry went back to town, travelling late by moonlight in the car of a friend. He had to attend a conference early the next day. Margaret and the children and her friend Helen were now alone.

They spent the long days bathing and sunning themselves, and in the evenings they left the children and climbed to the downs at the back of the town and lay to watch the moon come up far out to sea; the turf was soft and the nights were warm.

Helen's old school-friend Phoebe lived in the little seaside town, and now that they were alone Phoebe often came to visit them, bringing her car.

Phoebe was a quiet girl, enjoying a private income and no cares.

They took the children for a picnic on the banks of the military canal far into the country where it turned inland from the coast three miles over the flats. From the banks of the canal that were covered with long grass and shaded by trees that were planted at the time the canal was built to keep Napoleon out, you could see the Martello towers that marked the line of the coast, and in the distance the pale sea that was as pale as the sky, baked clean of colour.

Helen wandered off on her own and explored the marshes which, cut by little sluggish streams, lay over towards the sea. The little quiet streams were like dykes, the water did not seem to move in them, the tall reeds stood up and every now and then a cow, mistaking the reedy margin for firm land, floundered in the soft mud. Swishing her tail the cow stood puzzled; the flies made a black patch over one eye which gave her a dissipated look.

Helen took off her shoes and walked barefoot over the soft marsh grass, and barefoot over the bare patches where the mud lay caked in squares. She sat down on the bank of the stream and looked up from below at the tall reeds and the thick bushes on the river-side. The cowparsley towered above her head as she sat close down by the water's edge. How hot and solitary it was here on the marsh by the river, and what a hot muddy watery cowparsley smell it had.

Helen fell into her favourite Brobdingnagian dream . . . if she were so high (say three inches) and the rest of the world unchanged, how very exciting and daring would be this afternoon excursion; each puddle a solitary lake, each tussock a grass mountain, the cowparsley mighty jungle trees, the grass, where it rose high by the river, to be cut through with a sharp knife for a pathway. Helen's enjoyment of scenery was as great as her friend Margaret's, but very different. She was rather childish about it and liked to imagine herself on some bold quest, travelling, with gun and compass and perhaps a fishing rod, exploring, enduring—for some reason, of course. But what reason? Ah, that she had never been able to determine. Never mind, it was the movement, and the sun and the grass and the lakes and the forests that made it exciting, and so agreeable. Sometimes there would come the steep face of a great inland cliff, and up the baked surface of its caked mud slopes the intrepid adventurer would slowly climb, hand over hand, step by step, half crawling, half climbing, the sun hot on her back. Until at last, and only just in time (for really it was hard work), she would come to the top and, pulling herself over by a fistful of tough grass most happily to hand, fling herself down on the grassy plateau, saying, 'Well, that's over, and not bad, if I may say so.'

Full of these agreeable fancies, soaked in sunshine and spattered with smelly mud, Helen now made her way back to where her friends were setting the tea-things on the river bank.

Hughie was grumbling and tossing. 'I hate this place,' he said, as Helen came up to them. 'I wish I was in London again; I would rather be in the Edgware Road. Do you hear, mother?—the Edgware Road.'

Helen sighed. She thought there must be something in Margaret's gentleness that drove her son mad. Hughie must wish to see her round on him, to make her angry, to make her cry?

'Do we have to have Hughie with us?' she said coldly.

One day Phoebe came again to fetch them in her car.

'Would you like to come to Dungeness?' she said. She wanted to go there herself, it would make a nice afternoon trip, and they could get some tea at the Ship Inn on the way.

'Would you like to come, Hughie?' she said.

'Yes,' said Hughie. 'No, I don't know. If it is fine I should like to bathe again.'

He ran off to spend some time jumping from the high stone wall on to the beach.

Anna lay in the shade of her mother's deck chair.

'My little seal,' said Helen, holding the painting water for her so that she could colour her drawings. She had a temperature and could not bathe or walk or ride.

'Shall we go to Dungeness?' said Phoebe lazily.

'I don't know. Shall we, yes, let's go quickly to Dungeness, now,' said Helen, jumping up. 'Let's take Anna because she can't ride or swim. Let's go quickly before anyone notices.' (She meant Hughie.)

Helen and Phoebe gave Margaret no time to think about it; the three girls and the child Anna ran laughing through the hotel and climbed into Phoebe's car—there was an exciting air of conspiracy.

'To Dungeness, to Dungeness,' sang Anna as the car leaped along.

There will be hell to pay, thought Helen glancing quickly at Margaret and away again.

'It is an escape,' she said, 'an escape from the men.' (From Hughie, she thought, from the restless son, the troubled father.) 'Hurrah. A car full of women is always an escaping party,' she said. The women laugh, their cheeks flush with excitement. They are off again, laughing they say, as they say of giggling schoolgirls, 'They're off again, that's set them off!' The boiled mutton is forgotten, the care of the children, the breadwinner's behest, the thought for others; it is an escape.

Phoebe drove with enthusiasm, well and quickly. Now the long line of bungalows gave way to black buildings of military significance, and now on their left, half out of the sea, stood up the great black wheel that had carried Pluto's cables, they were coming now to the home of Pluto and to the great lighthouse of Dungeness. Black barbed-wire curled over the landscape and ramshackle fishing huts straggled to the water's edge, with sparse dry grass growing up from the shingle gardens. The lighthouse establishments and the lighthouse itself were prinked and spry, untouched by the litter of war, bearing their neat fresh colours in stripes of grey, black, ochre and white.

They parked the car and made off through the barbed-wire entanglements to the brink of the sea at the very point of the land where it dropped to fathoms deep so that great ships drew safely close. They sat with their feet dipping in the sea, watching the porpoises at play and the seagulls dipping for fish. Where the North Sea met the Atlantic the waves drove up against each other, but in the lee of the land a great calm left the surface smooth to the winds' track.

Margaret began to be unhappy. She felt that she had been persuaded—over-persuaded—by these bold friends. Already the temperament of Hughie that was the temperament of his father Henry, stretched an accusing finger. They would certainly be late for dinner.

How beautiful the air was, how hot and singing and full of salt and dry. The sea was quite navy blue where the two seas met; out to sea lay a band of white mist: it was a heat haze. 'All through the war,' the lighthouse man had said, 'the lighthouse kept its light burning. Yes, they tried to bomb us once or twice, but then they gave it up, we were too useful to them, too.'

Yes, it was Pluto they were after, though they didn't know what it was, but just to be on the safe side; they'd hear rumours—oh no, they'd never got anything, except them bungalows.

'Margaret, dear,' said Helen, 'do cheer up. It won't do Hughie any harm; in fact, it will do him good.'

(Oh no, they did not understand.)

'The wife is the keeper of the peace,' laughed Helen, 'but take a long view, Margaret, the long peace is not always the peace of the moment. Hughie must learn.'

They were fifteen minutes late. Hughie met them with a speechless fury.

'I will explain, darling,' said Margaret. Hughie, who was quite pale with passion, would not speak to them, but began an affected conversation with the major's eldest child at the next table. ('Hallo, Helen,' said David the lover, 'hallo.')

Margaret and the two children slept in one room. After dinner Helen went up with them, and now Hughie began to speak.

'You are low, disgusting women,' he said in a low, fast voice getting louder. 'You are liars. I curse the day I was born.'

Hughie was beginning to enjoy himself now, he was beating himself into a great passion and Margaret was getting frightened. He went on in a mad voice: 'It is always Anna who must come first,' he said, 'always Anna, naturally Anna. Mother,' he shrieked, 'you have deliberately humiliated me to give me an inferiority complex to cripple me in my whole life; later I shall go mad, I feel that I am going mad now, and how will you like that, mother? The people will point to you in the street and they will say, "There is the woman who drove her son mad." ' He began to scream, 'Mad, mad, mad! When I am in an asylum you will be sorry.'

Helen picked up a rolled bundle of *Life* that had come from America. 'Shut up,' she said, and hit him sharply across the shin with the rolled magazine, 'shut up, you fool; whose car was it, anyway?'

'Anna is the second-born,' went on Hughie, 'she has displaced me in my mother's affection, as soon as she was born this is what she did.'

'You are practically word-perfect,' said Helen, with a fearful sneering expression. She hit him again. 'Stop putting on an act, shut up.'

At this moment the door opened and in walked Henry with his suitcase in his hand.

'Babies,' he said, 'babies, what hope have they? They are wheeled in prams along the sea-front like lords; often there is a coloured canopy between them and the sun. You can see them from the window, look.' He crossed the room and stepped out on to the balcony looking down at the sea walk. 'Look, it might be Lord Curzon. No wonder they are megalomaniacs. I've had a most difficult day,' he said, 'the people at the Clinic, really, it hardly seems worth while going on, really no idea . . . hum, hum, hum . . . ' (He began to sing under his breath.)

Suddenly everybody was talking at once.

Daddy, Hughie, Helen, Children, Mother, Anna . . . .

The words tumbled out all together at the same moment. Henry, washing his hands at the washbasin, did not seem to notice, he was still lost in thought for the babies he had seen in their prams along the promenade on his way from the station. 'Megalomaniacs,' he muttered.

'Well, good-bye,' said Helen, choking back the laughter that was now rising in hysterical gusts. 'I am staying the night with Phoebe you know. I'll see you all at breakfast. I'll be back for breakfast.'

She ran along the beach picking up some mussels as she ran. The moon was coming up in the twilight sky over to the horizon; but on the west there were long red and pink and green streaks where the sun had just settled below the hills: these were a dark soft olive green. She and Phoebe, Helen thought, could cook those mussels and have them for a late supper. One could always eat two suppers these lovely hungry seaside days. Oh, what a pleasant holiday this was, how much she had enjoyed today for instance; hitting Hughie had also been quite agreeable. How much she enjoyed the company, the conversation, her darling friend Margaret, the stormy Hughie, the sleek child Anna, and that excursion to Dungeness, and now dear Henry's unexpected return.

She sat down for a few minutes before turning inland across the fields to Phoebe's house. She sat on the beach by the tall posts of the breakwater where the sea was lapping up quickly to high tide again. The shingle was still warm on the surface with the day's sunshine, but underneath as she dug her fingers deeper it was cold and wet. She leant her head back against the post and closed her eyes and took a deep sniff of the sea-weedy salt smell, that had also some tar in it. Presently there would be the mussels for an extra supper with dear Phoebe, but not just yet, just for a time she could stay here. Helen shifted a bit from the post and lay flat back upon the beach, looking up at the sky. There was the sun and the moon (well, almost the sun) and the stars and the grey sky growing darker, and there was this fascinating smell, and on the other side of the breakwater the sea was already getting deep. If only the beach were really as empty as the moon, and she could stay here and lie out all night, and nobody pass by and no person pass again ever. But that no doubt was what it would be like when one was dead (this was always what Helen thought death was like), and then of course the poor soul would weep for its loneliness and try to comfort itself with the memory of past company. Was not that what Hadrian had been thinking so cold and solitary of the sheeted dead–*quæ nunc abibis in loca?* Best, then, to make best use of the company that was now at hand. Helen got up and walked slowly up the beach and across the fields towards Phoebe's house, pausing only for quite a short time to lean over the bridge that crossed the dark river, and only then because there was a fish swimming that came suddenly into the track of the moonlight, rising to snap at a mosquito that lay out late on the water.   *1949*

THE STORY OF A STORY

'I am so awfully stuck,' sighed Helen. 'You see it is a monologue, it is Bella's monologue, it is saying all the time how much she is thinking about Roland all the time, and thinking back, and remembering, and so on. It is like a squirrel in a cage, it goes round and round. And now I am stuck. Tell me, Ba, how can I come out of it to make a proper ending,—ah, that is difficult.'

The two girls were having lunch together in the Winter-garden, the potted palms were languid, but underneath the palms stood out like tropic flowers the keen dark faces of the yellow-skinned business men. Everybody was drinking strong bitter coffee that was served rather cold and soon became quite cold. The yellow of the skins and the yellow of the whites of the eyes of the business men spoke of too many of these cups of coffee drunk too often.

'You do not mean to say,' said Barbara, 'that you are writing a story about Roland and Bella?'

'Well, I am trying to,' said Helen, 'but it is very difficult, but I am doing my very best.' She sighed again. Oh, how difficult it was.

'But,' said Ba, 'you know that Roland will not like that.'

'Pooh, nonsense,' said Helen, 'he told me that he would not mind.

But it is so difficult, but difficult, always so difficult to write.' Helen sounded rather desperate. 'It must be right,' she said, 'quite right.'

'But Roland,' said Ba again.

Helen began to look rather dreamy. 'Human beings are very difficult,' she said. 'You know, it is like the lady in Maurice Baring, she was one of these foreign countesses he has, and she was sitting at dinner next to an English writer. "And vat is it you write about, Mr So-and-So?" she said. "Oh, people," he said, "people." "Ah, people," said the countess, "they are very difficult." '

'But Roland . . .' went on Ba.

'I do wish you would stop saying "But Roland," ' said Helen. 'I tell you Roland said to me, "Helen, I suppose you will write a story about us." And I said, "Well, perhaps I shall, but it is very difficult." "Well, do," said Roland. "write whatever you like Helen, I shan't mind." '

'Ah,' said Ba, 'he only said that to trap you.'

'No, no,' said Helen, 'he could not be so base.'

That evening Ba tidied herself and went round to see Roland and Bella. Bella was not very pleased to see her. Bella was a warm-hearted person, but this girl was rather tiresome, she was *devoted* to Roland.

'I think I ought to tell you,' said Ba, 'that Helen is writing a story about you.'

This is how the war broke out, the war that was to carry so much away with it, the personal war, the war that is so trivial and so deadly.

Bella loved Helen.

'Oh, Helen, how could you do such a thing?'

'What thing is that, Bella?'

'Why, to write a story about Roland and me.'

'Oh, that,' said Helen, 'why that is very difficult. I am so terribly stuck, you know. It is difficult.'

'But Roland . . .' said Bella.

'How is Roland?' said Helen. Helen admired Roland very much for his fine intelligence, and because this fine intelligence was of the legalistic variety, very different from Helen's.

'Roland is furious,' said Bella, 'simply furious.'

'It is so frightfully difficult,' said Helen, 'to get it exactly right.'

'He says that if you do not give him your word that you will not publish the story he will not see you again.' Bella was now in tears, she loved Helen and she loved Roland. 'It is all so difficult,' she said, 'and Ba with her student-girl devotion does not help, and this story makes it all so difficult.'

'Yes, yes,' said Helen, 'it is difficult. I am most frightfully stuck.'

'You mean you are going on,' wept Bella. 'Oh Helen, how can you?'

'Well, that is just it, I do not know that I can. But,' said Helen, 'I shall try.'

'But Roland says . . . '

'Pooh, *that*. He cannot be so stupid.'

The two friends walked together across Hyde Park to Hyde Park Corner. Coming down the long grass path between the trees towards the statue of the great Achilles, Helen saw a horse drawing a cart full of leaves and bushes. 'Oh look, Bella, look,' she said. The horse had broken into a gallop, he drew the cart swiftly after him. He was a tall heavy animal, dappled grey and white, his long flaxen hair flew in the wind behind him, the long pale hair streamed on the gale that was blowing up between the April trees.

'What is it,' said Bella, who was in the middle of saying something about Roland. 'Well, what is it?'

'That horse,' said Helen.

'How can you look at a horse at such a moment? You want it both ways,' said Bella.

Helen looked at Bella and laughed. 'It is the moment to look at a horse.'

She went home and went on with the story. It was building up slowly, it was not so bad now, it was coming right.

When she had finished it she took it round to Lopez, who was also a writer. Lopez was a very clever quick girl, she had a brilliant quick eye for people, conversations, and situations. She read the story right through without stopping. 'It is very good, Helen,' she said, and then she began to laugh.

When Helen had gone Lopez rang up all the friends, and the friends of the friends, the people who knew Lopez and who knew Helen, and who knew Bella and Roland, and even those who knew the devoted girl Ba.

'Look,' said Lopez, 'Helen has written a most amusing story about Roland and Bella. It is very amusing, exactly right, you know.'

Everybody was very pleased, and the soft laughter ran along

the ground like fire.

Cold and ferocious, Roland heard about it, coldly ferociously he sent messages to Helen. Bella came running, bringing the ferocious messages. 'Pentheus, ruler of this Theban land, I come from Kithairon where never melts the larding snow . . . ' Yes, it was like the Greek messengers who have the story in their mouths to tell it all. 'Where never melts the larding snow,' that was surely the cold Roland, so ferocious now and cold.

'He says,' cried Bella, 'that he will never see you again if you do not give him your word that never shall the story be published.'

'Pooh,' said Helen, 'we have heard about that. Very well then, I shall never see Roland again.' But she, too, began to cry. 'It is so easy,' she said, 'to close a door.'

'But he says,' went on Bella, 'that he will have his solicitor write to you, that he will have his secretary ring you up, that if the story is published he will at once bring a libel action against you.'

'It is so difficult to get these stories right,' said Helen, her thoughts moving off from Roland to the dear story that was now at last so right, so truly beautiful.

Bella shook her ferociously. 'Listen, Helen, he will bring a legal action.'

Helen began to cry more desperately and to wring her hands. 'He cannot be so base, indeed it is not possible, he cannot.' But now through the thoughts of the beautiful story, so right, so beautiful, broke the knowledge of the cold and ferocious Roland, that was now standing with a drawn sword.

'Ah, ah, ah,' sobbed Helen.

Bella put her arms round her. 'It is no good,' she said, 'no one and nobody has ever got the better of Roland.'

'But I love Roland,' said Helen, 'and I love you, and I even love the student girl Ba, and I love my story.'

'You want it both ways,' said Bella.

'There is no harm in this story,' wept Helen, 'and he is condemning it unseen. He has not seen it, it is soft and beautiful, not malicious, there is no harm in it and he is destroying it.'

'Roland,' said Bella, 'is a very subtle person, he is this important and subtle character.'

'For all that,' said Helen, 'he does not understand, he does not understand one thing, or know one thing to know it properly. He is this legalistic person.'

'He is the finest QC of them all,' said Bella.

'He knows nothing,' said Helen, and at once her thoughts passed from the benign and the happy, to the furtive, the careful, the purposeful and the defensive.

'You are childish about this story,' said Bella.

'You shall see that I am not.'

'What are you thinking of now?' said Bella, watching Helen and watching the ferocious intent expression on her face.

'I am thinking of Baron Friedrich von Hügel,' said Helen.

'Eh, who might he be, and what are you thinking about him?'

'I am thinking of what he said.'

'And what did he say?'

Helen screwed up her face and spat out the words, the terrible judging words. 'He said, "Nothing can be more certain than that great mental powers can be accompanied by emptiness or depravity of heart." He was thinking of Roland, be sure of it.'

Helen went home and knelt down and prayed, 'Oh, God,' et cetera. She was a Christian of the neo-Platonic school. She prayed that she might do the right thing about the story. This matter that had been so trivial was now running deep, deep and devilish swift. It was time to pray. She prayed that all might come right between herself and Roland and her dear friend, Bella. She knelt for a long time thinking, but it did not seem the right thing to do to suppress the story because of the threat of legal action and for the fear of it. But she knew that Roland could have no idea of this, he could have no idea of Helen but the idea that she was a friend of Bella's, a rattle, a literary girl, a desperate character, a person of no right sense or decency. 'But I will go on with it,' said Helen, and she began to cry again, and said, 'It will be the death of me.' For now the human feelings were running very swiftly indeed, and on the black surface of the hurrying water was the foam fleck of hatred and contempt.

She did not see Roland because she would not give him her word. Driven by Bella, whose one thought was that the story should not be published, because of the trouble that would follow, Helen cried, 'I will give my word in contempt, using his own weapon, for my word shall mean as much as his word meant when he said, "Write about us, write what you like, I shall not mind." '

Bella felt that her heart would break, the violence and the obstinancy of Roland and Helen would break it quite in two.

'He denies that he ever said such a thing.'

'But Bella, you heard him. You were coming out of the bathroom carrying the goldfish. You heard him, you told me that you heard him.'

'I heard him say, "Go ahead, write what you like," but it was a threat.'

Helen began to choke. 'It was no threat, he spoke most friendly, very open he was, he was treating me as a friend, he was anxious that it should be right.' She sighed and smiled and gave Bella a hug. 'It was difficult, but now it is right.'

She did not see Roland, but still she saw her dear friend, Bella. But always Bella was telling her of the affair, *Roland versus Helen*, and how the situation lay, and what Roland had said only yesterday, and what the part was that the girl Ba was playing.

The weeks went by, the story was now accepted and to be published. Nobody had seen the story as it now was, worked upon and altered with cunning and furtiveness and care and ferocity, it was now a different story, hedged and pared from legal action, but as good as it had ever been, good, shining bright, true, beautiful, but pared from legal action.

Helen prayed that the story might come safely through. The friends said that Roland would not bring an action, that he would not do it, that he was playing a game of bluff to frighten Helen, to make her withdraw the story.

But now Helen had the thought that she was dealing with a maniac, *a person who would go to all lengths.*

The danger of the situation and the care for it made her grow thin, and every time that she saw Bella the harsh cruel words of Roland were repeated, and what Ba had said was repeated, and all of it again, and again; and then again.

'Ba says that it is a good thing that she has done informing against you,' said Bella, 'for in this way the story will not be published, and everybody's feelings will be spared.'

'But the feelings and truth of the story will not be spared,' said Helen, and a bitter look came across her face. 'That does not matter I suppose?'

Bella tore on, 'Roland was saying only yesterday, "Helen will have to write a story to say how the story was not published," and he laughed then and said, "Helen must be taught a lesson," and he said, "Now that she has learnt her lesson I am willing to see her again." '

Helen put her head on the tablecloth of the restaurant where they were having lunch and wept, and she said: 'I wish Roland was dead.'

It was now Good Friday. Restlessly, sadly, Helen moved about the wide empty garden. The sun shone down through the fine ash trees and the lawn was bright green after the heavy rain. What a terrible day Good Friday is as the hour of twelve o'clock draws near. Her Aunt was at ante-communion, her sister at the mass of the pre-sanctified, but Helen would not go to church because she had said, 'I wish he was dead.' She went into the garden to fetch the book that she liked to read on Good Fridays and read:

> *The third hour's deafened with the cry*
> *Of crucify Him, crucify.*
> *So goes the vote, nor ask them why,*
> *Live Barabbas and let God die.*
> *But there is wit in wrath and they will try*
> *A Hail more cruel than their crucify.*
> *For while in sport he wears a spiteful crown,*
> *The serious showers along his decent face run slowly down.*

She thought of the crucifixion that was now at twelve o'clock taking place, and she thought that she, in her hatred of Roland and her con-tempt for him (because of the violence of the law that he threatened to use) had a part among the crucifiers, and she wept and hid her face, kneeling against the cold bark of the fine ash tree. 'The cruelties of past centuries are in our bones,' she cried, 'and we wish to ignore the sufferings of Christ, for we have too much of a hand in them. Oh I do not wish Roland dead, but what is the use to love him and to love my dear Bella? They will not receive it and the door is now closed. But even now,' she said, 'if I withdraw the story, and give my word that neither here nor in America—(for it was not only British Rights that Roland was asking her to give up)—shall the story be published, nor after his death, will that door be opened again and shall I be received? Oh, no, no'—Helen screamed and twisted and beat her head against the cold ash tree bark—'I cannot do this, and if I did never could it be the same between us, for it would be the act of a slave person, and no good thing.' And she knelt at the foot of the fine ash tree and prayed, 'Come, peace of God,' et cetera.

She went into the house and fetched out her writing pad and wrote to Bella: 'Dearest Bella, I think we had better not see each other for a bit. I like to think agreeably of you and Roland and even Ba, but I cannot do this now while I am seeing you, so we had better not see each other.' She paused and then went on, 'We can think of each other in the past as if we were dead.' Helen's face brightened at this idea, 'Yes, as if we were dead. So with love to you and Roland and Ba.'

When she had written her letter she thought, 'One must pay out everything, but it is not happy.' She thought of Bella's beautiful house and the beautiful pictures that Roland had collected, especially there was such a beautiful picture in the hall, the Elsheimer, ah, that was it, *it was the gem of his collection.* Helen wept to think that never again would she see her dear friends, Roland and Bella, in love and friendship, and never again would she see the beautiful house, the Elsheimer, the trees in the shady garden or the goldfish swimming in their square glass tank. She thought that she must pay out everything and she supposed that the Grünewald prints that Roland had lent her must now also be given back.

She fell asleep in the garden and dreamt that she was standing up in court accused of treachery, blasphemy, theft and conduct prejudicial to discipline. Roland was cross-examining her:

'Do you think it is immoral to write about people?'

'No no, it is very difficult.' She held out her hands to Bella and Roland, but they turned from her.

'You go into houses under cover of friendship and steal away the words that are spoken.'

'Oh, it is difficult, so difficult, one cannot remember them, the words run away; when most one wants the word, it is gone.'

'You do not think it is immoral to write about people?'

'It is a spiritual truth, it is that.'

The dream-girl breaks down under cross-examination by the cold and ferocious Roland. She is cross, lost and indistinct.

'The story is beautiful and truthful,' she cries. 'It is a spiritual truth.'

The girl cries and stammers and reads from a book that she draws from her pocket, 'Spiritual things are spiritually discerned, the carnal mind cannot know the things of the spirit.' She weeps and stammers, 'Of the Idea of the Good there is nothing that can be spoken directly.'

21

The dream-girl glances furiously upon the Judge, the Counsels for Defence and Prosecution, upon the tightly packed friends, who have come to see what is going on. She reads again. 'Let those be silent about the beauty of noble conduct who have never cared for such things, nor let those speak of the splendour of virtue who have never known the face of justice or temperance.'

There was now a mighty uproar in the court, but the dream-girl cries out high above the clamour, stuttering and stammering and weeping bitterly, and still reading from her book, 'Such things may be known by those who have eyes to see, the rest it would fill with contempt in a manner by no means pleasing, or with a lofty and vain presumption, as though they had learnt something grand.'

'He that hath yores to yore,' said the Judge, 'let him yore.' And he pronounced the sentence, 'You are to be taken to the place from whence you came . . .' The police constable and the wardress in the dock beside her took hold of her.

On the Tuesday after Easter there was a letter from Bella. 'How could you lump me with Ba?' she wrote.

Helen sat in her office, here were the proofs of the story come by post for correction. How fresh and remote it read, *there was no harm in it.*

Her employer, who was a publisher, came into the room where she was sitting. 'What's the matter, Helen?' he said, seeing the tears running down her cheeks.

She told him the story of the story.

'Look here, Helen,' said the employer, 'just you cut them right out, publish the story, tell him to go to hell.' Then he said, 'I am afraid the editor will have to be told.'

The moment, which had been so smiling when the employer first spoke, now showed its teeth. 'Of course, I don't expect he'll mind,' he said. But mind he would, thought Helen.

She took the bath towel from the drawer in her desk and held it in front of her face. 'The law of libel,' she said in a low faint voice, 'is something that one does not care to think about.' She pressed the towel against her face. 'It is everything that there is of tyranny and prevention.'

'Yes, yes,' said the employer, and walking over to the mantelpiece he pinched the dead lilac flowers that were hanging down from the jam jar, 'Yes.'

Helen wrote to the editor to tell him. He regretted that in the circumstances he could not publish the story.

When Helen got the editor's letter she wrapped the raincoat that Bella had given her tightly about her and walked along the rain swept avenue that led to the park. She sat by the bright pink peony flowers and she thought that her thoughts were murderous, for the combination of anger and impotence is murderous, and this time it was no longer Good Friday and the soft feeling of repentance and sorrow did not come to drive out the hatred. The rain fell like spears upon the dark green leaves of the peony plants and the lake water at a distance lay open to their thrust. It was not enough to know that the door against Roland and Bella was now locked tight, she must forget that there had ever been such people, or a door that was open to be shut. But how long would it take to forget, ah, how long, ah, that would be a long time.

1946

GETTING RID OF SADIE

'Crumbs,' said my brother, 'if this isn't old Sadie. No, seriously, old girl, just look here. Well, isn't it?' He threw the paper across to me.

We were sitting—it is some time ago now—in the old playroom at Staithe overlooking the bay—and a good deal nearer to it since the last winter's landslide. You could have tossed the ash-tray spit into Skeddles Wash.

'What?' I said, 'where?' Edward came across and jabbed a finger. 'There.' It was a short paragraph and said that Miss Elizabeth Findlater, aged fifty, had been convicted 'of attempting to extort money by menaces.'

'It was a day like this, too,' I said, when we could speak for gaping, 'the day of our famous dress rehearsal, our *plot* . . . sunny, with the wind blowing hard off the sea . . .'

Did we remember?—did we not. We were about ten and fourteen at the time, Eddy rather grown-up and sick to have to spend eight weeks' holiday in Aunt Slippy's house (as it was then) with only two beastly girls, myself and cousin Beth, for company.

Oh, and the governess, Miss Elizabeth Findlater.

'She's a sadist,' Eddy said to me on our second day there, 'you wouldn't know what that means but it's being cruel and liking it.'

And he began to thump and sing, 'Sadist-Sadie, You are a shady lady . . . ha, ha, ha.'

'Look out, you fathead, she'll hear you.'

'Not a chance, anyway she likes us.'

As a matter of fact, she did, perhaps because we weren't frightened of her. Like poor Beth. Perhaps again, and the glum thought dogs us still, because she thought we were more 'her sort'.

'She *beats* her,' I said. 'Fancy being beaten by a governess.'

'And she isn't a lady anyway, she's just a common old bag.'

'She's a bag, she's a hag. All the same, we can't have a relation of ours being banged about by a bag of a hag who isn't a lady.'

We turned solemn then thinking of poor Beth.

'It's awful in every way,' I said, 'because, well, it isn't only beating, though that's simply awful . . . .'

Eddy struck in. 'Girls aren't beaten, they're not, it's just not civilized.'

'Oh shut up. Well,' I went on, 'that couldn't be worse, but also you know she's got Beth absolutely dumb with fright, oh it's sickening. Old Sadie just plays cat and mouse with her.'

'It's the power complex,' said Eddy.

'Do you know the other day,' I said, 'I found Beth crying in the corner by the banisters and do you know what it was? Sadie had sent her to fetch her spectacles from her bedroom and Beth couldn't find them. And all the time they were in Sadie's ghastly reticule thing.

'I'd seen them as I ran past to go upstairs, the reticule hung open on Sadie's lap. She must have *known*. And when I got upstairs there was Beth crying and shivering, it was awful, like poor old Prince when he's going to be sick.'

(Prince was the dog, a heavenly old Labrador we all adored.)

Well, that settled it. Sadie had got to be got rid of.

Of course, you might have thought Beth could have told her mother, our Aunt Slippy—that is if you hadn't known Aunt Slippy.

She was one of those females who care for nothing but horses, never spoke to Beth and paid the governess to keep her out of the way. Also she was hardly ever there.

We supposed she was out with the horses (wrongly, as it turned out, but that comes later). Anyway Beth's case, poor, tormented, sweet Beth's horrible case, obviously lay in our hands. What could we do?

We had endless confabulations, Eddy and I, and meanwhile time was running short.

'Sadie likes us,' I remember saying, 'she does like us, Eddy, so we'd better work on that.'

Well, we did. We played up to Sadie, we flattered her, we told her she was 'different', 'such a brick' you know, 'a sport', etcetera.

The old thing (she was quite forty, I suppose) really came on wonderfully. Oh, she liked it, lapped it up and asked for more.

It was finding the passbook that finally hatched out our plot.

'I say, look here, Eddy,' I said, 'old Sadie's got £700 on current account.'

It may seem odd that an infant of ten should know about passbooks and current accounts, but our dear father had ideas about education and especially about giving a practical turn to arithmetic lessons by linking them up with cheque books and company promotion and so on, and not a bad idea either.

'Crumbs,' said Eddy (as he still does), 'that's a lot for a governess –and on current account.'

The plan we finally decided on was really rather clever. I still think it was, though Eddy says it was too complicated and couldn't have worked out.

We were going to persuade old Sadie to accompany us on a picnic to Skeddles Wash some afternoon–that is almost any afternoon–when poor Beth was being 'kept in' doing long division sums for a punishment (she never mastered the Italian method though heaven knows we toiled to teach her).

The cliffs at Skeddles Wash run up sheer in a sharp-angled cleft with a cave at the end and another on top of it at the back and a fairly sticky climb up to it, which would flatter Sadie's vanity–'So different' you see, 'such a sport' (well, she was pretty agile for her age)– and an even stickier climb out to the cliff which only I could do because it got so narrow.

At high tide the lower cave would be ten feet deep in water.

Well, the plan was for Eddy to tie Sadie's wrists as he was helping her up (he was huge even at fourteen, and she was barely five feet and skinny), then we'd tie her feet, too, and keep her there till the tide ran high.

Well, after that it really wouldn't have been difficult. We'd stick her up for £400. If she jibbed at writing the cheque (we'd have pinched the cheque-book from her bag, she always carried it around with her)–cash, of course, and a covering note to the bank requesting payment in one pound notes–we'd simply threaten to untie her and push her into the cave, we knew she couldn't swim–and that would be that.

Oh, she'd write the cheque, we were sure of that, and I'd hare off with it up the cliff, get Beth to take it to the bank, as she was always being made to do these dog errands and they knew her there, then I'd post the money in an old chocolate box or something to our London house addressed to myself 'To Await Arrival'.

(Daddy was most punctilious about our letters and there was only about a week to go by now.)

Oh, we'd thought of everything—even to getting the bank's receipt signed by Sadie, though we guessed some more of the water threat would be necessary here. Our point was this—Sadie would get the £400 back when she'd got herself another job.

(We put that in because we didn't want her getting the money and turning up again.)

Well, as I say, that was the plan. It was a bright, sunny day with a strong north-easter blowing when we staged our dress rehearsal. Eddy insisted on a dress rehearsal, with careful timing for the high tide, and dear old Prince, the Labrador, who weighed about a ton, was to 'stand in' for Sadie.

Dear old dog, it was Prince who sent things wrong. We were hauling him into the upper cave, with a handkerchief tied round his front paws, when the poor old boy began to make the most extraordinary noises.

We let him down again, and Eddy jumped down, too, and then poor Prince was most terribly sick—he was always being sick but this was different, somehow, it was absolutely frightful, we thought he was going to die.

Eddy went deathly white and I was crying.

We carried the old man home and got the vet and as a matter of fact he was his own sloppy, sweet self in a day or two and nothing to show for it.

But that was the end of the great plot to get rid of Sadie. Because —and this is where Aunt Slippy comes in again. Apparently she *had* been thinking of something besides horses, she'd been thinking of a chap called Captain Harry Satterthwaite.

Well, the upshot was that Daddy bought the house and Aunt Slippy went off with this Satterthwaite person to somewhere in America where he had a ranch (he'd been staying with nearby friends of Aunt Slippy's on a stock-buying visit).

So Beth went to boarding-school and spent her holidays with us, and Sadie, our Sadie, 'Miss Elizabeth Findlater,' off she went too and not a squeak was heard of her till this cutting turned up, to bring

27

it all back again, our plot, our bloodthirsty, perfectly criminal plot.

Sitting now, ten years after, in the old playroom, I said to Eddy, 'You know even if it didn't come off, we meant it to, we would have enjoyed threatening her.'

I turned to the cutting again. '. . . extorting money by menaces.'

'Perhaps we were rather alike, us and her.'

'I've often thought that,' said Eddy. 'It's the thing that's kept me straight.'

So we couldn't help laughing then, yes, in a way it finished in laughter. But not for Sadie, no, not for Sadie.

'Well,' I went on, answering this thought that must have been in both our minds, 'she was a cruel beast, wasn't she? It would just have been a case of one cruel beast meeting two cruel beasts, too bad. And I don't think we would really have pushed her in.'

'I wouldn't count on it,' said Edward glumly.

'Well, I don't suppose it would have been *necessary*.'

My brother squinted slightly, pushed to the point.

'I wouldn't count on that, either,' he said.

1955

SURROUNDED BY
CHILDREN

Under the shadow of the trees in Hyde Park the mothers are nursing the babies, and in the long grass of Kensington Gardens and on the banks of the Serpentine the sisters are caring for the brothers, under the trees the aunt walks. What is the aunt doing, under the trees walking? She is thinking of the young man who has the ice-cream vendor's cart; the cart of the ice-cream vendor is upon the road, he is peddling briskly away from the walking aunt.

The brothers of the sisters and the babies of the mothers have no care at all; theirs is a careless fate, to be pampered and cared for, no matter if there is no money the brothers will have the sisters to jump around after them, the babies will have the mothers to nurse them, the aunt will have the pleasure of sweet dreams under the tree and the ice-cream vendor will have his escape upon the saddle of his bicycle cart.

It is a pleasant English summer's day in the Gardens and in the Park. The brother of the sister has an ice-cream which he is eating, it is plastered upon his mouth, it is all over his whole face; he relishes the ice-cream. The sister anxiously combs back from her brow with long soiled finger the lank lock; she is worried to keep at the same time an eye upon the eater of the ice-cream and upon the younger brother who will paddle in the Serpentine, nobody shall say him no.

The little brothers and sisters who are the children of rich parents play also in the Park, but their play is watched by ferocious nannas. The children are fat and pink-cheeked but listless rather at their pleasures; their voices are the high-class English voices, the baby accents of the ruling classes, the clichés too, already they are there, a little affected is it not? and sad, too, that already the children are so self-aware almost already at a caricature of themselves—'we are having fun.' 'Did you enjoy your walk in the Park?' says Mama upon the child's return. 'Why, yes, it was fun you know, just rather fun. Did we enjoy the walk Priscilla?' Priscilla sneers with tight lips above baby teeth. 'Why yes, I suppose so, it was fun, rather fun.'

Towards both these groups of children is now coming a famously ugly old girl, she has wisps of grey hair carelessly dyed that is rioting out from under her queer hat, as she walks she mutters to herself. Very different is the walking dream of the old girl from the walking dream of the love of the ice-cream vendor. Ah, upon the old girl is no eligible imagination for the nurture of a love-life of entertainment value. As she walks she talks, and also her hands that are delicate and long, like delicate long birds' claws, clasp the air about her. She fetches up to a standstill beneath the rich chestnut tree; in the shadow of the tree is reposed a grand pram for a rich child. The pram is empty but the covers are turned back. How invitingly securely rich is the interior of this equipage that is for a grand infant of immensely rich parentage, how inviting indeed the interior where the covers lie backwards upon the pram beneath the green tree!

The famously ugly old girl is transfixed by this seducing vision of an open and deserted perambulator, she will get into it, come what may that is what she will do, that is her thought. Her hands now stretch upward to remove the queer hat to fling it down upon the grass, the toque lies at her feet. Tearing apart the lapels of her tightly buttoned coat she will not wait, the flimsy bombazine tears, the coat is off; with one hand she props herself against the dear perambulator, kicks shoe from shoe, stands stockingfoot.

But now the children gather round, close in upon her fast, for what is going on here? The children of the rich parents and the children of the poor parents are now united in a childish laughter, the sisters of the brothers have forgotten their care, the nephews and nieces of the aunt are here, the rich children have escaped their nannas, laughing and staring they close in upon the poor old girl, they join hands and laugh.

'Ah,' cries the sad beldame, transfixed in grotesque crucifixion upon the perambulator, stabbing at herself with a hatpin of the old fashion so that a little antique blood may fall upon the frilly pillow of the immaculate vehicle, 'what fate is this, what nightmare more *agaçant* so to lie and so to die, in great pain, surrounded by children.'

1939

30

TO SCHOOL IN GERMANY

How much harm may one do at 16—being egotistical, argumentative, infantine of heart being then, absolutely, 'oneself at 16'? This begins as a comic story, a summer anecdote of not much account. How far it thrust into the future casting shadows I do not even know; perhaps I am flattering my 16-year-old self thinking she thrust into the future at all.

At 16 I was at school in Potsdam. Infantine of heart I may have been, even for a schoolgirl, but I was beginning to have a faint inkling of how extremely inconsistent one can be and how little difference it makes to one's comfort, opinions and behaviour having this brought home. As it was, almost daily.

For we were an international lot at Fraulein Plotzler's academy and opinions ran strong. There was, for instance, my friend Steppy. Steppy was an American of Polish ancestry. The cause which had our public voice—hers and mine—was a lofty internationalism, but this did not prevent fights between us at a lower level.

'We beat you British.' 'You were in Poland at that time grinding the faces of the poor.' 'America beat Britain.' '. . . or slinking in the Ghetto. They were British on both sides, bar the Hessians on ours.'

'Slinking in the Ghetto?' 'Ha, ha, how can you pretend to be liberal when you won't even speak to Flossie Silbermann?' 'She is a Jewess.' And so on.

Yes, at sixteen I was disputatious rather than sentimental and it was in nothing at all of a sentimental mood that I went to spend the holidays, as often I did, with some friends of my mother, the von Rs.

This 'R.' name has since become rather notorious, so let the initial stand. Herr von R. was 'a nice old thing' (forty-five I dare say), of a humour more Berlinish than East Prussian. His wife was asthmatic, but self-effacing, there was a daughter, Bella, and there was Maxi. That summer was wonderfully hot and long. Maxi, Bella and I used to go riding and bathing in the shallow Baltic that I liked so much, and sailing too.

Maxi was in his first year in the university and liked holding forth. He was dreadfully taken up with those historico-hysterical pseudo philosophical ideas one used to laugh at then, not guessing what was coming up out of them, or wanting to guess.

At mealtimes he did not say much, because German sons, even

student sons, did not talk when their fathers were there. But on the rides and bathes Maxi would grow very extreme indeed about the Jews and about how cynical, corrupt, of poor moral fibre and generally disgusting the English were.

Bella took no part in these arguments; she was a calm girl and thought only of catching shrimps and pounding them into a paste which she wolfed down on slabs of cold toast.

'She has no mind,' Maxi used to say, 'but she is very pretty.' There was a great deal of tension between Maxi and me. But it was not on my side—or at all, I thought—a sentimental tension of the sort that so comically drives engaged couples to dispute with violence some trivial question, say of party politics.

It was all the same unnerving; 'worse than Steppy' I used to think, quite often ferocious. And as the names Maxi cast at me of persons the English were supposed to have mistreated or bamboozled meant little to me or positively nothing, I spent much time in Herr von R's library looking up an answer for him. But by then, of course, he had gone on to something else.

Maxi was a handsome-looking boy, I could see that, but my mind was on other things. So one day when he suggested we should go off together and leave Bella in the kitchen with her shrimps, I sighed a little, thinking of the arguments to come up, but said yes.

You know those inland seas that lie behind the strips of coast up by Pillau getting on for Koenigsberg? The von Rs' land lay there, the great flat fields running by the lakesides down to the sand dunes and the sea.

At once Maxi began to speak of the Jews again. 'Oh, heavens, Maxi, not again.' And I said there were moments when one liked to be quiet and think. And that this was such a beautiful day, so hot and still, we should do better to enjoy it in silence, and swim silently, rather than for ever to rattle round those hackneyed exascerbating and wicked sentiments vis-à-vis the Jews, the English or any other persons, institutions or opinions.

And as we strolled together through the pinewoods towards the sea shore I began to have some curious thoughts—as for instance that a fine sunny day can make one feel more separate than ever, especially if one's companion is in a frame of mind noticeably different from one's own, for there the creature is in the physical lump, the disturbed playmate, and how on earth can one wrap oneself from him?

'I am trying not to be aggressive,' I said, 'I am really very fond of you, Maxi; I don't want to be cross because it is such a hot day and just the day for a swim and soon I shall be going back to England, so do not be so beastly cross.'

And to cheer him up I began to read out aloud from a letter I had had from my sister Elizabeth who was still at school in England.

I sighed as I read. I had been in Germany for more than a year now and would be glad to go home. 'Isn't it marvellous,' Elizabeth wrote, 'Ocean Swell and Ephesus beating Teheran? I'm simply thrilled. And I'm terribly pleased about Dicky Boy, he's a very nice-tempered horse and of a queer spotty colour. I'm simply dumbfounded, Ian has got engaged to Caroline, much to Nat's disgust. I can't get over it. Must dry up now, tons of love though.'

I looked up. Maxi was looking quite extraordinary, his eyes very odd, boiled slightly and bursting and his face of a most peculiar shade of dark red. 'I don't believe you've heard a word I've been reading.' I was going to walk off aloofly and get the picnic things out when Maxi leapt at me. 'Don't you know I love you?'

'No I don't,' I said. 'Heavens, you must be stark staring mad. I mean I didn't. I think it's soppy all that, all right for Caroline I dare say. What on earth's the matter?'

'Don't you love me at all?' 'Well, Well, I never thought about it. (Oh do shut up.) I'm very fond of you. I'm fond of Bella too and I think your father is heaven and . . .'

But I stopped because of the way Maxi was looking. 'I say, you aren't serious, I suppose? I say, look out, you'll break my arm.'

He got a grip on my plaits and pulled my head back. 'I say, look out, you're pulling my hair. Maxi, do shut up!'

He began to shout that he loved me, that he was serious and wanted to marry me. 'But we can't' I said, 'we're not old enough.' 'We could be engaged.' 'I know I'm not in love with you, Maxi (oh, do shut up!) and I couldn't marry you, anyway. I've nothing against it in principle but it wouldn't work.'

'Why not?' So out it came with nothing much more behind it than crossness for a spoiled day you might say and yet—was it not for me at that moment a sort of truthfulness, the summing up of a situation? 'Why not?' 'Because you're German.'

I wish I might say I never saw Maxi again and so leave it as a summer anecdote. But I did see him again, many years later and in dreadful circumstances. It was after the war in a restaurant in the British Zone not far from Berlin. I was with my cousin Eustace, who was in the Army. We went into this restaurant and it was very crowded. We sat down at a table in the corner. There was one other person there, a thin, twisted-looking oldish man.

Only when he looked up with those blue eyes of old did I recognise this person for Maxi.

'Good heavens, Maxi!' I cried and turned to Eustace.

'This is Maxi von R. you know, I stayed with them ages ago; in another world.'

My cousin stiffened up at the name von R.

'I could make a bolt for it, I suppose,' said Maxi with a quite ghastly smile. 'I don't think I should,' said Eustace. Maxi turned to me.

'He's not got it quite right, has he?' and then in an echo that fell from a long way off, in a thin mincing false voice that came as my own voice from a long ago afternoon in East Prussia he said: 'I've nothing against it in principle but it wouldn't work.' My cousin took him off then. Maxi was a war criminal on the run. I had guessed that, of course. Later, Eustace told me his record. It was vile beyond words.

'Don't worry,' he said when I told him the summer story, 'if it hadn't been that it would have been something else.' I stared at the coffee in the bottom of my grubby cup. 'How beastly and bitter it all is: I hate this "holier than thou" situation we are all in now.' 'We ARE holier than him,' said my cousin.

Maxi got 15 years.

1955

34

THE HERRIOTS

When the Herriots first went to Bottle Green to live it was in the wicked old spacious days of King Edward. Dr Climax went his rounds in a carriage and pair; he wore a silk top hat and had a manner that was agreeable and distinct. Everybody in Bottle Green hired a maidservant, and the better families had two and called them by their surnames.

It is now after the war. At number 54 Colefax Gardens there lives this family of Herriots. They are well connected 'you know' on their father's side, coming down from Sir Edward Coke the Great Chief Justice. The eldest son is called Coke, he pronounces it 'coak'—Coke Herriot.

Bottle Green is now a very large suburb. The Greek bankers have sold their landed estates to speculative builders who have made a good thing out of it. They have built rows of small houses. The sons and fathers of the families who live in these new small houses are no longer lawyers and stockbrokers, they are clerks and commercial travellers.

But in an old tall house at number 13 The Pound (this is where the old cattle pound still stands) lives Peg Lawless and her aged great-aunt, Mrs Boyle. There is another aunt also living there, a Miss Cator, Peg's mama's sister. The parents of this child are both dead. She has been brought up in a way that does not appeal to some people in the suburb.

Old Mrs Boyle felt every now and then that Peg should be taught how to keep house, but Miss Cator, who was affectionate and impatient, preferred to do it herself, and about this there was always disagreement between the two ladies.

When Peg was a child she used to play with the Herriot children. One day she was coming home from school when a schoolboy pulled her hair. Coke Herriot was coming along behind, Peg ran back and said: 'Please fight that boy, Coke.' Coke punched the boy's nose and it began to bleed.

Coke was seven years older than Peg and passed straight from the VI form into the Army. One day when Peg was twelve Coke came round in his officer's uniform. Peg was in trouble at home with Mrs Boyle. Mrs Boyle had won a battle against Miss Cator and Peg had been sent out to buy three bloaters. She was an absent-minded child and brought home in the shopping basket three lobsters instead of three bloaters. Peg had a sort of absent-mindedness that worked in a queer way. Always between lobster and bloater there was this indecision. She said lobster and saw bloater. Her great aunt was exasperated, although in a way it was a support for her argument that Peg should have more housekeeping practice. She was a splendid rigid old lady with old fashioned ideas about discipline. She was talking in the sitting room with Coke when Peg came in. 'You deserve a good whipping,' she said. Peg was putting a log of wood on the fire and Coke wanted to help her but as he touched her arm she stumbled, dropped the log and would have fallen, but Coke caught her and she fell on to his knees. He put his arm round her and laughed: 'Shall *I* whip you?' he said.

When Peg was eighteen she married Coke. He had given up his commission (he could not live on the pay) and taken a job in the City; it was the most foolish thing he could have done, the office work irked him and the orders fell off. No good, he gave it up and became a salesman in cars for a time. He had an adventurous streak in him and would have made a career in the army—if there had been a war. He lost his salesman's job and went back to the City. He hated the work but could do nothing else. He was not clever; he was warm-hearted and affectionate and quick-tempered.

Peg and he had so little money that when the first baby was coming they had to give up their flat and go and live with Mrs Herriot. (Old Mrs Boyle was dead and Miss Cator had gone to keep house for a married brother with an invalid wife.) They had a room on the ground floor, a bedroom at the top of the house and of course the 'use' of the bathroom and kitchen. Peg fretted at first, they could do nothing with the house, it was awful. Instead of their beautiful fresh seersucker curtains they had the old people's Nottingham lace curtains looped back with olive green silk sashes.

Peg was absent-minded and not good with money and now she felt that the happy feminine-independent days of her childhood were over indeed. Mrs Herriot unquestioningly put the wishes of the men first. Peg had been brought up to think that men were to fetch and to carry. She felt that she had married into an Indian or Turkish family. But she loved Coke and Coke loved her. As the baby got nearer Peg began to have nightmares about the Indian-Turkish idea and the curtains.

When the baby was born it was a lovely boy with bright blue eyes like Coke's. They adored the baby and used to play with him up in the bedroom on the ugly old-fashioned bed.

Mrs Herriot had not the buoyant temperament of Mrs Boyle and Miss Cator, she was depressed and she had the idea that Coke's shift-lessness was Peg's fault. When the baby was teething it used to cry a great deal. Mrs Herriot would come upstairs and open the door and sigh and go out again. Peg was very anxious and overwrought. One day she was rather rude to Mrs Herriot. 'Do not come in here,' she said. 'Please go away.' When Coke came home Mrs Herriot complained to him. Coke was very tired and dispirited after a long day at the 'terrible' office and he was cross with Peg. She would not say anything, she looked desperate. It drove him mad. He struck her.

Peg had nowhere to go to get away from them. She wandered round the house distraught. She looked into the sitting room, old Mr Herriot was reading his paper. Mrs Herriot was in their room, looking for something. Peg went into the scullery (they had no maid now) and began to do the vegetables for dinner. She began to cry; now that she was alone she could think again. She thought that Coke had struck her but that if they could go away it would be all right.

Coke and Peg went to church on Sunday to take the baby to be christened. He was called James after his uncle—James Coke Herriot. The vicar was a practical kind wise man, very much one with his parishioners. The church had always been the centre of the life of Bottle Green, but until a few years ago they had had a scholarly eccentric vicar called Mr d'Aurevilly Cole. He was not married and became so eccentric that he had to retire. When he retired he married the organist; the ladies of the parish had always thought he would marry her. The London papers had a paragraph about it—'Vicar marries organist after twenty years'.

The present vicar was not so much a 'recluse' (they said) as Mr Cole, but he was splendid with the people, hard-working and sensible. Everybody helped everybody. At the church it was a very happy community.

But when the people came home so many of them were like old Mr and Mrs Herriot and Peg and Coke. The big houses of the pre-War period were let out in flats, nobody could get away from anybody, there were always nerve storms and people crying themselves to sleep, but also laughing when there was some money and the little cars could go along.

After the christening people made a good appearance, and the vicar came back to the Herriots to tea. Everybody's secret—it was no secret in the family that Peg and Coke had quarrels and that Coke had struck her—was put away; Mrs Herriot had excellent hostess manners, the tea came in on a trolley. They were so poor by now that the family had margarine, but butter was given to the vicar and the friends.

Peg and Coke had a sleepless night after the christening. The baby cried and cried. Peg nursed the baby and tried to quieten him. Coke called to her. She put the baby down and got into bed. She put her arms round Coke and pressed her hands over his ears so that he might not hear the baby. He began to cry, too, his head against Peg's shoulder.

One day Coke came home very cock-a-hoop. He had met an old friend who was running a flash amusement park in the poorer part of Bottle Green. 'I'm giving up my job at the office, Peg,' said Coke, 'I told old Snooks exactly what I thought of him. You ought to have seen his face.' 'Oh, Coke, what are we going to do now?' 'Trust me, dear old girl, Tommy is a good chap, and he knows what's what. I'm going into the fun fair business with him.'

To begin with there was a lot more money. Peg went out and about with Coke and Tommy. Tommy was a dashing sort and used to come to the house and flirt with Mrs Herriot. He had vulgar hearty manners and Mrs Herriot would never have had him in the house if she had not thought it might help Coke. One day Tommy came round and found Peg alone. 'Peg,' he said, 'I'm hard up, I must have £20, it's a dead cert. I can pay it back next Friday, but if I don't get it now it's all up with the business.' Peg gave him £20 out of the tin box where Mr Herriot kept his papers.

There was no more news of Tommy and the men came round and shut up the fun fair, and came round to the Herriots to see Coke. Peg was in disgrace. They were so poor now with Coke out of a job that there was very little food in the house and they could not afford a fire.

On Sunday morning very early Peg went to church. She prayed that she might find some work to do to help Coke. She cooked the Sunday dinner. It was eaten in silence, there was a little soup and some cheese and bread, afterwards she made some tea. They sat in the sitting-room for a time behind the lace curtains, and then Peg and Coke went upstairs. It was very cold in the bedroom, the baby was quiet now, sleeping in his cot. Coke sat in the armchair with Peg in his arms. She fell asleep with her head on his shoulder. She dreamed about Bottle Green. She was walking along and round. She knocked at all the doors down a long street, at each door there was a woman who answered the bell. There was no conversation between them, only gestures. A refusal, and the door was closed. Inside each house there were little rooms. The rooms were the homes of the people. There were old ladies and gentlemen, nodding on separate chairs; there were young married couples with babies, the babies were crying, the women were laughing sometimes and talking with their husbands; sometimes they were silent and angry.

At the end of the street there was a tall house with a flight of steps leading to the front door. In her dream Peg knocked and knocked. There was no answer. It was number 101.

When Peg woke up she kissed Coke and put on her hat and coat. 'Where are you going, Peg?' 'Just out for a few moments, darling Coke, I won't be long.'

She went to the house at number 101. It was kept by an old lady who was very eccentric; she gave Peg a job as companion at £1 a week.

Coke was left at home all day; he went off sometimes in the morning early, he walked round and round the streets looking for work. Mr and Mrs Herriot were very quiet now; there was no conversation.

The old lady at number 101 began to be in love with Peg. Every day she made her take her to the cemetery. There they sat; the old lady, Mrs Barlow, talked to Peg, holding her hand: 'When I am dead I shall be laid out in a beautiful white dress, the candles will burn round my head, you will kneel there at the foot of my couch. I shall be laid on a beautiful couch. You will pull down the blinds and kneel there by the light of the candles. That will be for me the greatest moment. And you will be with me.'

'I must go home now, Mrs Barlow, my baby must be fed, I have my baby to see to. Will you let me go now?'

'Not yet, wait a little while, it is only dusk, wait till the light fails.' Then she said: 'You must bring the baby to see me. We shall get on well, the little rogue, next time you come you must bring him.'

When Peg got home that night Coke said: 'Peg I am a poor sort of failure, how can you love me, I am no good to you at all, I might as well be dead.'

'If only we could get away,' said Peg, 'life would be so different. But I love Bottle Green so much, too; sometimes I think I could *not* go away, but always I say this: If we could get away. It is the sort of thing one says, nothing really.'

'I don't wish to go away either,' said Coke.

The next day Mrs Barlow said to Peg: 'Your husband has not found work yet?' 'No, but he is happier now and quieter in his mind. I think his father will find some sort of work for him where he is. He is an old man now and must retire soon. Perhaps Coke could have his place.' 'You are happy here with me?' 'Yes, very happy.' 'You, too, feel easier in your mind since you have been with me?' 'Yes, I feel so quiet too, and happy. I used to feel if I could get away from Bottle Green I should then be happy. But now I do not wish to go away.' 'Coke will have his job, you will see. And now we must go, we shall be late for the cemetery.'

They went up to the cemetery and sat on a seat beneath the yew tree. Mrs Barlow said: 'It is very vulgar to think in the absurd terms "you can get away". There is only one way in which you can get away, in the lofty and ethereal conception of the aristocrat, and that is to die and be buried.'

At this moment Coke came through the cemetery gates. His face was lit up like a flame. He came straight towards them and pulled Peg to her feet. 'How do you do, Mrs Barlow?' he said. 'Darling Peg, it is all right, I have got the job of travelling plumber, father is going to retire at the end of the month.' Mrs Barlow began to cry, 'I am so happy,' she said. Peg and Coke sat down on each side of her, and Coke gave her some chocolate he had bought for the baby.

1939

40

SUNDAY AT HOME

Ivor was a gigantic man; forty, yellow-haired, gray of face. He had been wounded in a bomb experiment, he was a brilliant scientist.

Often he felt himself to be a lost man. Fishing the home water with his favourite fly Coronal, he would say to himself, 'I am a lost man.'

But he had an excellent sardonic wit, and in company knew very well how to present himself as a man perfectly at home in the world.

He was spending this Sunday morning sitting in his bedroom reading Colonel Wanlip's 'Can Fish Think?' letter in ANGLING. '. . . the fallacious theory known as Behaviourism.'

As the doodle bomb came sailing overhead, he stepped into the airing cupboard and sighed heavily. He could hear his wife's voice from the sitting room, a childish, unhappy voice, strained (as usual) to the point of tears.

'All I ask' sang out Ivor, 'is a little peace and quiet; an agreeable wife, a wife who is pleasant to my friends; one who occasionally has the room swept, the breakfast prepared, and the expensive bric-a-brac of our cultivated landlord—*dusted*. I am after all a fairly easy fellow.'

'I can't go on' roared Glory. She waved her arms in the air and paced the sitting room table round and round.

Crump, crump, went the doodle bomb, getting nearer.

'Then why,' inquired Ivor from the cupboard (where he sat because the doodle bombs reminded him of the experiment) 'did you come back to me?'

Glory's arms at shoulder height dropped to her side. There was in this hopeless and graceful gesture something of the classic Helen, pacing the walls of Troy, high above the frozen blood and stench of Scamander Plain. Ten years of futile war. Heavens, how much longer.

She ran to the cupboard and beat with her fists upon the door. 'You ask that, you . . . you . . . you . . . '

'Why yes, dear girl, I do. Indeed I do ask just that. Why did you come back to me?'

'Yesterday in the fish queue . . . ' began Glory. But it was no use. No use to tell Ivor what Friedl had said to her in the fish queue . . . before all those people . . . the harsh, cruel words. No, it was no use.

The doodle bomb now cut out. Glory burst into tears and finished lamely, 'I never thought it was going to be like this.'

Crash. Now it was down. Three streets away perhaps. There was a clatter of glass as the gold-fish bowl fell off the mantlepiece. Weeping bitterly Glory knelt to scoop the fish into a half-full saucepan of water that was standing in the fender.

'They are freshwater fish' said Ivor, stepping from the cupboard.

Glory went into the kitchen and sat down in front of the cooking stove. How terrible it all was. Her fine brown hair fell over her eyes and sadly the tears fell down.

She picked up the french beans and began to slice them. Now it would have to be lunch very soon. And then some more washing up. And Mrs Dip never turned up on Friday. And the stove was covered with grease.

From the sitting room came the sound of the typewriter. 'Oh God' cried Glory, and buried her head in her arms, 'Oh God.'

Humming a little tune to himself, Ivor worked quickly upon a theme he was finishing. 'Soh, me, doh, soh, me. How happy, how happy to be wrapped in science from the worst that fate and females could do.'

'If only I had science to wrap myself up in' said poor Glory, and fell to thinking what she would wish, if she could wish one thing to have it granted. 'I should wish' she said, 'that I had science to wrap myself up in. But I have nothing. I love Ivor, I never see him, never have him, never talk to him, but that the science is wrapping him round. And the educated conversation of the clever girls. Oh God.'

Glory was not an educated girl, in the way that the Research Persons Baba and Friedl, were educated girls. They could talk in the informed light manner that Ivor loved (in spite of Friedl's awful accent.) But she could not. Her feelings were too much for her; indeed too much.

'I do not believe in your specialist new world, where everybody is so intelligent and everybody is so equal and everybody works and the progress goes on getting more and more progressive,' said Glory crossly to Friedl one day. She shook her head and added darkly, 'There must be sin and suffering, you'll see.'

'Good God, Glory,' said Ivor, 'you sound like the Pythoness. Sin and suffering, ottotottoi; the old bundle at the cross roads. Dreams, dreams. And now I suppose we shall have the waterworks again.'

'Too true,' said Friedl, as again Glory fled weeping.

'Sin and suffering,' she cried now to herself, counting the grease drips down the white front of the stove. 'Sin, pain, death, hell; despair and die. The brassy new world, the brassy hard-voiced young women. And underneath, the cold cold stone.'

Why only the other day, coming from her Aunt's at Tetbury, there in the carriage was a group of superior schoolgirls all of the age of about sixteen. But what sixteen-year-olds, God, what terrible children. They were talking about their exams. 'Oh, Delia darling, it was brilliant of you to think of that. Wasn't it brilliant of Delia, Lois? But then I always say Delia is the seventeenth century, if-you-see-what-I-mean. And what fun for dear old Bolt that you actually remembered to quote her own foul poem on Strafford. No, not boring a bit, darling, but sweet and clever of you—especially sweet.'

At the memory of this atrocious conversation between the false and terrible children, Glory's sobs rose to a roar, so that Ivor, at pause in his theme, heard her and came storming into the kitchen.

'You are a lazy, slovenly, uncontrolled female,' he said, 'You are a barbarian. I am going out.'

'Round to Friedl's, round to Friedl's, round to Friedl's,' sang out Glory.

'Friedl is a civilised woman. I appreciate civilised conversation.' Ivor stood over Glory and laughed. 'I shall be out to lunch.'

He took his hat and went out.

'The beans,' yelled Glory, 'all those french beans.' But it was no good, he was gone.

Glory went to the telephone and rang up Greta.

Greta was lying in bed and thinking about hell and crying and thinking that hell is the continuation of policy. She thought about the times and the wars and the 'scientific use of force' that was the enemy's practique. She thought that evil was indivisible and growing fast. She thought that every trifling evil thing she did was but another drop of sustenance for the evil to lap up and grow fat on. Oh, how fat it was growing.

'Zing,' went the telephone, and downstairs padded Greta, mopping at her nose with a chiffon scarf which by a fortunate chance was in the pocket of her dressing gown. The thought of the evil was upon her, and the thought that death itself is no escape from it.

'Oh yes, Glory, oh yes.' (She would go to lunch with Glory.)

The meat was overcooked and the beans were undercooked. The two friends brought their plates of food into the sitting room and turned the gas fire up. Two of the asbestos props were broken, the room felt cold and damp.

'It is cold,' said Greta. 'Glory,' she said, 'I like your dressing gown with the burn down the front and the grease spots, somehow that is right, and the beastly dark room is right, and the dust upon the antique rare ornaments; the dust, and the saucepan with the goldfish in it, and the overcooked meat and the undercooked beans, it is right; it is an abandonment. It is what the world deserves.'

'Let us have some cocoa afterwards,' said Glory.

'Yes, cocoa, that is right too.'

They began to laugh. Cocoa *was* the thing.

'When you rang up,' said Greta, 'I was thinking, I said, Hell is the continuation of policy. And I was thinking that even death is not the end of it. You know, Glory, there is something frightening about the Christian idea, sometimes it is frightening.' She combed her hair through her fingers.

'I don't know,' said Glory, 'I never think about it.'

'The plodding on and on,' went on Greta, 'the de-moting and the up-grading; the marks and the punishments and the smugness.'

'Like school?' said Glory, waking up a bit to the idea.

'Yes, like school. And no freedom so that a person might stretch himself out. Never, never, never; not even in death; oh most of all not then.'

'I believe in mortality,' said Glory flippantly, 'I shall have on my tombstone, "In the confident hope of Mortality". If death is not the end,' she said, an uneasy note in her voice, 'then indeed

44

there is nowhere to look.'

'When I was studying the Coptics,' said Greta, 'do you know what I found?'

'No, Greta, what was that?'

'It was the Angels and the Red Clay. The angels came one by one to the Red Clay and coaxed it saying that it should stand up and be Man, and that if the Red Clay would do this it should have the ups and downs, and the good fortune and the bad fortune, and all falling haphazard, so that no one might say when it should be this and when that, but no matter, for this the Red Clay should stand up at once and be Man. But, No, said the Red Clay, No, it was not good enough.'

Glory's attention moved off from the Coptics and fastened again upon the problem of Ivor and herself. Oh dear, oh dear. And sadly the tears fell down.

Greta glanced at her severely. 'You should divorce Ivor,' she said.

'I've no grounds,' wailed Glory, 'not since I came back to him.'

'Then you should provoke him to strangle you,' said Greta, who wished to get on with her story. 'That should not be difficult,' she said, 'And then you can divorce him for cruelty.'

'But I love Ivor,' said Glory, 'I don't want to divorce him.'

'Well, make up your mind. As I was saying,' said Greta, '. . . . . so then came the Third Angel. "And what have you got to say for yourself?" said the Red Clay, "What have you to promise me?" "I am Death," said the Angel, "and death is the end." So at this up and jumps the Red Clay at once and becomes Man.'

'Oh Glory,' said Greta, when she had finished this recital, and paused a moment while the long tide of evil swept in again upon her, 'Oh Glory, I cannot bear the evil, and the cruelty, and the scientific use of force, and the evil.' She screwed her napkin into a twist, and wrung the hem of it, that was already torn, quite off. 'I do not feel that I can go on.'

At these grand familiar words Glory began to cry afresh, and Greta was crying too. For there lay the slop on the carpet where the goldfish had been, and there stood the saucepan with the fish resting languid upon the bottom, and there too was the dust and the dirt, and now the plates also, with the congealed mutton fat close upon them.

'Oh do put some more water in the fish pan,' sobbed Greta.

Glory picked up the pan and ran across the room with it to take it to the kitchen tap. But now the front door, that was apt to jam, opened with a burst, and Ivor fell into the room.

'They were both out,' he said. 'I suppose you have eaten all the lunch? Oh, hello Greta.'

'Listen,' said Glory, 'there's another bomb coming.'

Ivor went into the cupboard.

'Do you know Ivor,' screamed Greta through the closed door, 'I had a dream and when I woke up I was saying, "Hell is the continuation of policy".'

'You girls fill your heads with a lot of bosh.'

Glory said, 'There's some bread and cheese in the kitchen, we are keeping the cocoa hot. Greta' she said, 'was telling me about the Coptics.'

'Eh?' said Ivor.

'Oh do take those fish out and give them some more water,' said Greta.

'The story about the Angels and the Red Clay.'

'Spurious,' yelled Ivor, 'all bosh. But how on earth did you get hold of the manuscript, Greta, it's very rare.'

'I don't think there's much in it,' said Glory, 'nothing to make you cry. Come, cheer up Greta. I say Ivor, the doodle has gone off towards the town, you can come out now.'

Ivor came out looking very cheerful. 'I tell you what, Greta,' he said, 'I'll show you my new plastic bait.' He took the brightly coloured monsters out of their tin and brought them to her on a plate. 'I use these for pike,' he said.

There was now in the room a feeling of loving kindness and peace. Greta fetched the cheese and bread from the kitchen and Glory poured the hot cocoa. 'There is nothing like industry, control, affection and discipline,' said Greta.

The sun came round to the french windows and struck through the glass pane at the straw stuffing that was hanging down from the belly of the sofa.

'Oh, look,' said Glory, pointing to the patch of sunlight underneath, 'there is the button you lost.'

Silence fell upon them in the sun-spiked room. Silently, happily, they went on with their lunch. The only sound now in the room was the faint sizzle of the cocoa against the side of the jug (that was set too close to the fire and soon must crack) and the far off bark of the dog Sultan, happy with his rats.

1949

A VERY
PLEASANT EVENING

Helen darling I am so glad to see you, Lisa ran up the steps and kissed Helen, it was so long since she had seen her the last time in Cambridge at the Newnham Senior Student's Party, or was it at Professor Lichtenstein's at Oxford, that time Rudi upset the custard? Dear Helen, never would Lisa forget her dear friend. And now here was Helen in London suddenly, staying with the Hicksons in Moon Street, W.

Behind Helen in the wide Regency doorway stood a man. This must be Mr Hickson, but no of course he was dead. Helen introduced Mr Rambeloid. Oh yes of course, Anita Hickson had married again. How do you do, How do you do. Roland Rambeloid took them into the sitting room of the old grand but rather empty house. We are hardly settled in yet, he said, We have as you see very little furniture, we expect to get the rest out soon, but I expect it will be rather smashed up. Oh dear, the bomb, yes. But, said Lisa, you will be able to get an emergency supply with special permits. Oh yes, said Helen, but it all takes so long. I am so glad you escaped with your life, said Lisa. Roland Rambeloid looked rather startled, Oh thank you, thank you, yes, my wife and I as a matter of fact were at the play when it happened, it was Richard the Third.

They were now sitting drinking some pre-war sherry and some Irish whisky. How did you manage to save the sherry and the whisky? asked Lisa. Oh well, as a matter of fact we only borrowed this house from a friend. Oh yes, thank you, I will have some more whisky. How jolly good of your friends it was. Would you like to come down and see the cellar? asked Roland Rambeloid. You two run along, said Helen, I'll stay here, I have some buttons to sew on. She took some piles of mending and some reels of thread from under the cushion on the couch and a needle from the ashtray, and sat down again to sew.

You see, said Roland, prancing down the basement steps, this is such a fine old house, such wide shallow steps, on the main staircase I mean of course, steady now, mind this corner, there's a step out here and the light is off. Down they went. In the basement was a wide cool old kitchen where Anita Rambeloid, formerly Hickson, *née* exactly what Lisa forgot though she had been at college with her, was

47

cooking the dinner. How nice it smells, said Lisa, slipping a tomato into her pocket and advancing to the stove where Anita was boiling a stew. Run along, said Anita laughing, show her the cellar and the coal house Roland, off with you. What a happy house it was. Won't you have a tomato Lisa, said Roland, I may call you Lisa, mayn't I?

For dinner they had potato soup, Irish stew, a chocolate pudding with some frozen milk from the frig, some sardines on toast and black coffee laced strongly with the Irish whisky. There was also some Stilton cheese. We found this in the cellar, said Roland, pour some whisky into it, Lisa. The talk now turned to dialectical materialism. After the war, said Roland, England will be of no importance whatever, there will be only America and Russia, but we shall have our famous character of course, he went on hurriedly, seeing that his wife who was very pro-English was about to speak, And so we shall always suppose we amount to something, so everybody will be pleased.

Helen threw a Berkleyan remark into the conversation, fearing that it might lose its Cambridge flavour and become vulgar. Nonsense nonsense, said Roland, just words, baby-talk. If a man falls off a cliff in the dark because he cannot see it that is a proof that the world exists apart from the mind's thought of it, said Lisa. They had some more whisky. Well, Lisa went on, he does not know the cliff is there and yet it is there with a vengeance, it is the death of him. Helen's husband who had done little up to the moment except sniff took up the conversation, but it was now time to turn on the radio and listen to the budget speech. Practically everything they had eaten and drunk was to be taxed double, Roland looked hungrily at the Stilton. It is better to parcel it out slowly I think really, said Lisa, it would only make you sick, and with care it will last a very long time. Jolly nice of our friends, said Roland absentmindedly.

Lisa had some more whisky and went and sat by Helen and took her hand and asked, How are the children, how is Caroline, and how is Clorinda and how is Sarah? The children all had these smart Cambridge names, everybody of that age in Cambridge had these names. Nothing common like Doris, said Lisa. The sea mouse, said Helen's husband, and began to talk about the kangaroo and the young kangaroo that is, he said, born a worm. How can that be, said Lisa, a worm. No the kangaroo, it is like this, he is born with his claws and his fur on, but he is not quite finished off yet for all that, so the mother puts the child kangaroo into her pouch . . . or poosh, said

Roland rather irritatingly. Well, she puts the child into her pouch then the child kangaroo keeps warm and grows finished; it is attached to the mother kangaroo by some attachment of a sort, so that she can run and jump and leap without a fear that her child will fall out. Nonsense, said Helen's husband, it is a worm and from the worm it grows to the young kangaroo. Helen said hurriedly that no doubt the term worm was used in the widest sense. Oh I see, said Lisa, the worm, the way the mediaeval people used the word, it might be the dragon that Guy of Warwick hunted. Or the worm of the bible that dieth not, said Roland, or the worm of Milton that tempted the fairest of her daughters Eve. The mediaeval people were very imaginative, said Helen's husband, with a precise child's imagination, very visual. 'Spiritual ambition and imaginative loves,' said Lisa pat, for she felt there was about to be a quotation game and she would get in early. Helen's husband sniffed loudly, but Roland was pleased, he liked to talk about poetry in this easy gamey way. He said that he allowed himself to doubt whether any writer writing poetry to-day would so many centuries from now as we are from Milton be quoted easy by easy reading people apart from the research hounds.

Anita got up to go and fetch some more coffee. When she got to the glass door leading through into the garden and through again to the backstairs there was a bright red flash in the sky over the wrecked low rubble of Heartbright Street. Roland, she cried out, that must be a doodle. Roland looked at his stop watch and counted out the seconds, nobody spoke. He had got up to forty-five before the crash came. The house shook and the glasshouse windows fell out with a crack. Oh dear, said Anita, that happened only last month, we had them put back but we shall never get them done again, old Bonesey slipped them in for us on the quiet because Roland helped his son to get into the Blue Coat School, she sighed. She said that old Bonesey had now had a bomb on his house and had gone to live with his brother-in-law at Peckham.

Roland looked at the red skyline and said that it was awfully like the skyline in the last war with the red light now fading dark over Heartbright Street. He was restless to get back to his poetry. In the last war, he said, I used to sit in my dugout and read Childe Roland to the Dark Tower Came, nobody reads Browning nowadays, he looked in a challenging way at Lisa but went on quickly, Childe Roland is such an exact spiritual description of the detail of the

Flanders battlefield, he sighed, the bits of broken machinery, and the mud and the dampness and the greyness and the longness and the horse. He fell into a muse. Lisa took Helen's hand and said: One stiff grey horse his every bone astare, stood stupified however he came there, thrust out past service from the devil's stud, With that red gaunt and collopped neck astrain and shut eyes underneath a rusty main, seldom went such grotesqueness with such woe, I never saw a beast I hated so, He must be wicked to deserve such pain. Helen thought Lisa was getting rather drunk, What is that? she said. Lisa looked at Roland, It is Childe Roland, she said. The Victorian age, she said, for Roland was looking at her rather closely, Was a great age, a very great age, she laughed thinking that this was what old fashioned people said when old fashioned people died, A very great age. It would be surprising, she said if we should be so great as that. Well, said Roland grudgingly, that is rather like Childe Roland, but it is not quite right of course. No, said Lisa, the lines do not seem to have come right, they are not quite in the right order perhaps. I have my school Browning at home. She remembered the book quite well, it was congealed ox-blood red with gold embossing and on the fly leaf was written 'With love from Daddy.' Inside there was a bookmark with the word 'No' embroidered at the top and then an embroidered cross, and then the word 'No' again and underneath an embroidered crown.

Now, she said, I must go home. Roland said he would fetch her to the tube station. Good-bye Anita, good-bye Helen. Roland led off by a short cut through the back streets to the tube station. You are not cold, Lisa? No, no, not at all thank you. In the dark patch outside the lighted tube station Roland fell suddenly upon Lisa and began to kiss her. Oh Roland, how furious you are, sighed Lisa, as he gasped and panted. His right arm went round to the back of her shoulder, he caught hold of her hair and took a pull at it, forcing her head back, it was a furious adroit grip. Lisa began to laugh, Oh Roland, she said, and put her arms round him and kissed him, Now I must go. Lisa fell away from him and walked into the bright light of the station, but Roland came after her and took her in his arms and began to kiss her again under the bright lights and the approving eyes of the friendly porters. Good-bye Roland dear, Lisa drew apart and shook him politely by the hand, Thank you for a very pleasant evening.

1946

CATS IN COLOUR

Most of the pussycats in this beautiful picture book are little deb creatures, sweet little catsy-watsies of family, offspring of prize-winners and prizewinners themselves, 'daughters' (and sons) 'of the game'; the game in this case not being Shakespeare's Ulysses' game, as you will find it in *Troilus and Cressida*, when that cunning Greek general, in highranking Army company, refuses to kiss Cressida, because she is too easy by half, too much everyman's armful.

No, here 'the game', though not to my mind entirely removed from a hidden tartiness, is the game that human beings have been playing with the animal world since the first dog owned a human master and the first cat settled down upon a human hearth. It is we who have made these little catsy-watsies so sweet, have dressed them up and set them up, in their cultivated coats and many markings, and thrown our own human love upon them and with it our own egocentricity and ambition. I should have liked some little common cats alongside our beauties, some ash-cats going sorrowful about the palings of a poor London street, and not only for contrast with the beauties but for the truth of it as to the whole cat nature. Or is the cat-nature disguised as much by misery as it is by grandeur? And what in heaven's name is the cat-nature? Does it shine in the pretty eyes of our cat gathering in this sumptuous book, or is that a humanisation too? Really to look in an animal's eyes is to be aware of stupidity, so blank and shining these eyes are, so cold. It is mind that lights the human eyes, but what mind have animals? We do not know, and as we do not like not to know, we make up stories about them, give our own feelings and thoughts to our poor pets, and then turn in disgust, if they catch, as they do sometimes, something of our own fevers and unquietness. Tamed animals can grow neurotic, as the Colonel in a poem I wrote knew but too well (he was in India, hunting tiger):

> *Wild creatures' eyes, the colonel said,*
> *Are innocent and fathomless*
> *And when I look at them I see*
> *That they are not aware of me*
> *And oh I find and oh I bless*
> *A comfort in this emptiness*
> *They only see me when they want*
> *To pounce upon me at the hunt;*
> *But in the tame variety*
> *There couches an anxiety*
> *As if they yearned, yet knew not what*
> *They yearned for, nor they yearned for not.*
> *And so my dog would look at me*
> *And it was pitiful to see*
> *Such love and such dependency.*
> *The human heart is not at ease*
> *With animals that look like these.*

But I think all animal life, tamed or wild, the cat life, the dog life and the tiger life alike, are hidden from us and protected by darkness, they are too dark for us to read. We may read our pets' bellies and their passions, we may feed them and give them warmth; or, if we are villains, we may kick them out, ill treat them, torture them as heretics, as was done with witches' poor cats in the middle ages, worship them for gods, as Old Egypt worshipped them, put words into their mouths, like Dick's cat and the Marquis of Carrabas's sly pet. But still they are not ours, to possess and know, they belong to another world and from that world and its strange obediences no human being can steal them away. It is a thought that cheers one up.

I have written many poems about cats. I like cats, I like the look of them, I like the feel of a soft fat kitchen cat that folds boneless in one's arms. I could crush a fine cat. I wrote this short poem to express such a feeling. It is called 'When I hold in my arms a soft and crushable animal, and feel the soft fur beat for fear, and the fine feather, I cannot feel unhappy'; then the poem comes, just two lines, 'In his fur the animal rode and in his fur he strove/And oh it filled my heart, my heart, it filled my heart with love'. There is a bird mentioned there, but it is the cat-feeling that prevails. And do not be alarmed. The docile pet will turn if the pressure annoys him, out come the beautiful claws; our pet is not unarmed.

I had a cat once called Tizdal, just such a kitchen fat cat as I love. I wrote this poem about Tizdal, to show the love one can have for an animal, the love that likes to hug and stroke and tickle—and pinch lightly on the sly too, half-mocking, a love that says, Don't get too big for your boots, my little catsy-watsy Emperor-animal. I called it 'Nodding'; you'll have had this mood often yourself:

NODDING

Tizdal my beautiful cat
Lies on the old rag mat
In front of the kitchen fire.
Outside the night is black.

The great fat cat
Lies with his paws under him
His whiskers twitch in a dream,
He is slumbering.

The clock on the mantlepiece
Ticks unevenly, tic toc, tic-toc,
Good heavens what is the matter
With the kitchen clock?

Outside an owl hunts,
Hee hee hee hee,
Hunting in the Old Park
From his snowy tree.
What on earth can he find in the park tonight,
It is so wintry?

Now the fire burns suddenly too hot
Tizdal gets up to move,
Why should such an animal
Provoke our love?

The twigs from the elder bush
Are tapping on the window pane
As the wind sets them tapping,
Now the tapping begins again.

One laughs on a night like this
In a room half firelight half dark
With a great lump of a cat
Moving on the hearth,
And the twigs tapping quick,
And the owl in an absolute fit
One laughs supposing creation
Pays for its long plodding
Simply by coming to this—
Cat, night, fire—and a girl nodding.

Why should such an animal provoke our love? It was the indifference of course, the beastly, truly beastly—that is as appertaining to beasts —indifference of poor dear Tizdal I so relished. There is something about the limitless inability of a beast to meet us on human ground, that cannot but pique, and by pique attract; at least if we are in the mood for it, perhaps, at the moment, too thronged by too-ready human responses, sick of the nerves and whining of our own human situation *vis-à-vis* our fellow mortals. At such a moment the Cat-Fact lifts the human mind and relieves its pressures. As little girls love their dolls, so we love our pets. And use them quite often (I am afraid this is all too common, especially if we suffer from feelings of loneliness) as a stick to beat our human companions, who fail us in some way, are not affectionate enough, do not 'understand' us. How nice then to turn to the indifferent cat who can be made to mean so many things—and think them—being as it were a blank page on which to scrawl the hieroglyphics of our own grievance, bad temper and unhappiness, and scrawl also, of course, the desired sweet responses to these uncomfortable feelings.

I had an unlikeable elderly female cousin once and she had a very unlikeable cat; or perhaps we set the lady's own disagreeableness upon her cat, who was in himself I expect no better and no worse than any other animal. Fluff was this cat's name, and 'Fluff understands me' was my cousin's constant cry. Looking back from kindlier later years, I can only hope that my cantankerous old cousin's gullibility—for certainly Fluff cared nothing and understood nothing—went on being a comfort to her.

I like to see cats in movement. A galloping cat is a fine sight. See it cross the road in a streak, cursed by the drivers of motor cars and buses, dodging the butcher's bicycle, coming safe to the kerb and bellying under its home gate. See the cat at love, rolling with its sweetheart, up and over, with shriek and moan. But if a person comes by, they break away, sit separate upon a fence washing their faces—and might never have met at all. Better still to see this going on at night, as, if the moon is up and the roofs handy, you sometimes may. And what a wild cry they make, this moan and shriek on an ascending scale, how very wild the cat is then—very different, besotted cat-lovers may say, from 'our own dear Queen Cat's home life'. But there's not a prim beauty in this handsome book who is not capable of it and happy at it—provided of course our cats are whole cats and not 'fixed'. Alas, as D.H. Lawrence, in his ratty way, was always saying, so much of our modern life is 'fixed' and our animals are most 'fixed' of all. That is only one part of the sweetness and cruelty—and necessity too—of taking wild beasts and making pets of them.

Well, you may say, their lives without it were brutish and short. And has not dear Nip our own dear cat, just completed his seventeenth year in quiet peacefulness and jolly feeding, and enjoyed every moment of his life (well, has he?) though a doctored tom and firmly 'fixed' from kithood? Lawrence was a bit of a sentimentalist too, though in the opposite way from such doting cat fanciers as my late old cousin. But a bit of a sentimentalist in his idea of the satisfactions of animal life; I doubt for instance if the tomcat is ever satisfied; in the hands of Nature, sex is a tyrant's weapon.

I like to watch cats when they do not know they are being watched. Especially I like to watch them hunting . . . flies, perhaps, on the window pane—cat at fishpond, cat slinking with bird in mouth, cruel cat, cat stretching on tree bark to sharpen claws, then along the branch he goes to the fledglings' nest. Cat turning at bay, street-cornered by dogs. Scared cat.

Cats, by the way, for all their appearance of indifference and self-sufficiency are nervous creatures, all tamed animals are nervous, we have given them reason to be, not only by cruelty but by our love too, that presses upon them. They have not been able to be entirely indifferent to this and untouched by it.

Best of all, is the cat hunting. Then indeed it might be a tiger, and the grass it parts in passing, not our green English, or sooty town grass, but something high in the jungle, and sharp and yellow. But cats have come a long way from tigers, this tiger-strain is also something that can be romanticised. In Edinburgh's beautiful zoo, last summer with some children, I stopped outside the tiger's glass-bound cage. He was pacing narrowly, turning with a fine swing in a narrow turn. Very close to me he was, this glass-confinement needing no guard-rails. I looked in his cold eyes reading cruelty there and great coldness. Cruelty ? . . . is not this also a romanticism? To be cruel one must be self-conscious. Animals cannot be cruel, but he was I think hungry. To try it out, to see whether I—this splendid human 'I'—could impinge in any way upon this creature in his ante-prandial single-mindedness, I made a quick hissing panting sound, and loud, so that he must hear it—hahr, hahr, hahr, that sort of sound, but loud. At once the great creature paused in his pacing and stood for a moment with his cold eyes close to mine through the protecting glass (and glad I was to have it there). Then suddenly, with my 'hahrs' increasing in violence, this animal grows suddenly mad with anger. Ah then we see what a tiger—a pussycat too?—driven to it, can do with his animal nature and his passion. Up reared my tiger on his hind legs, teeth bared to the high gums, great mouth wide open on the gorge of his terrible throat. There, most beautifully balanced on his hind legs he stood, and danced a little too on these hind paws of his. His forepaws he waved in the air, and from each paw the poor captive claws scratched bare air and would rather have scratched me. This great moment made the afternoon for me, and for the children too and for my old friend, their mama (and for the tiger I daresay) and cosily at tea afterwards in Fullers we could still in mind's eye see our animal, stretched and dancing for anger.

Though pussycat has come so far down the line from his tiger ancestry, from jungle to hearthrug, or to those London graveyards where the grass grows 'as thin as hair in leprosy' as Browning put it, and where I have often seen tib and tom at work, there does still remain a relationship, something as between a Big Cat and a little one, that you will not find between cat big or little and a dog.

I will now tell you about a hunting cat I once observed. As I put this hunting cat scene in a novel I once wrote, I will if I may lift it straight from that novel as then it was fresh to me and if I told it over again it would not be. It was a hot day in summer, and I was swimming at the seaside with a cousin, not my elderly old lady cousin this time, but a boy cousin and a dear one, his name was Caz. So this is how it goes:

'We were now swimming above a sandbank some half mile or so out from the shore. Presently the sandbank broke surface and we climbed out and stood up on it. All around us was nothing but the sea and the sand and the hot still air. Look, I said, what is this coming? (It was a piece of wreckage that was turning round in the current by the sandbank and coming towards us.) Why, I said, it is a cat. And there sure enough, standing spitting upon the wooden spar was a young cat. We must get it in, said Caz, and stretched out to get it. But I saw that the cat was not spitting for the thought of its plight—so far from land, so likely to be drowned—but for a large sea-beetle that was marooned upon the spar with the cat, and that the cat was stalking and spitting at. First it backed from the beetle with its body arched and its tail stiff, then, lowering its belly to the spar, it crawled slowly towards the beetle, placing its paws carefully and with the claws well out. Why look, said Caz, its jaws are chattering. The chatter of the teeth of the hunting cat could now be heard as the spar came swinging in to the sandbank. Caz made a grab for the spar, but the young cat, its eyes dark with anger, pounced upon his hand and tore it right across. Caz let go with a start and the piece of wreckage swung off at right angles and was already far away upon the current. We could not have taken it with us, I said, that cat is fighting mad, he does not wish to be rescued, with his baleful eye and his angry teeth chattering at the hunt, he does not wish for security.'

How curious the observance of cats has been when great artists have been observing them, to paint and sculpture them, or work them in tapestry. The great early artists seem no happier with cats than they are with babies. Yet there is the cat for all to see, and the baby too. And do not say they extract the essence of cat or baby, because that they do not do. Did Raphael extract the essence of infants, in those stiff nativity little monsters, dropsical, wizened and already four years old though born but an hour ago? He did not, nor did Leonardo on his rocks, nor Dürer, nor anyone I can think of.

Who first among artists gave the essence and outline of infancy? . . . of cathood and doghood? Look at the Grecian cats and the Egyptian cats. To do so comfortably and without the need of visiting museums and libraries of ancient manuscripts, you should take a look at Christobel Aberconway's splendid compilation—*A Dictionary of Cat Lovers XV Century B.C. to XX Century A.D.*

It is not only the cats of antiquity that seem so peculiar (3,000 years may allow some difference in form) but . . . scaled to the size of a thin mouse, as we observe an Egyptian puss, couched beneath his master's chair? The Grecian cats, though better scaled, seem dull and the cats of our Christian era not much better. There is a horrible cat drawing in Topsell's *The Historie of Four-Footed Beastes*, dated 1607; there he sits, this cat, with a buboe on his hip, frozen and elaborate. In every line of this drawing, except for the cold sad eyes, the artist wrongs cathood. Quick sketchers do better, by luck perhaps. We all know Lear's drawings of his fat cat Foss. There is true cathood here, though much, too, of course, of Mr Lear, so 'pleasant to know'. Quick sketchers too can catch the cat in movement, and, though much addicted to, and fitted for, reclining, the cat moves—gallops, leaps, climbs and plays—with such elegance, one must have it so. Yet only this morning, I saw a cat quite motionless that looked so fine I could not have disturbed it. Hindways on, on top of a gray stone wall, its great haunches spred out beyond the wall's narrow ledge, this animal was a ball of animate ginger fur; no shape but a ball's, no head, no tail that was visible, had this old cat, but he caught all there was of winter sunshine and held it.

Why I particularly like Edward Lear's drawings of cat Foss, is one peculiar character they have that the cats of ancient Greece and Egypt, and our own Christian cats as shown by master painters, do not have. I mean that impression he gives of true cat-intransigeance, of the cat in its long drawn-out 'love-affair' with the human race—loved, mocked, cross and resisting. Why should we not mock our cats a little? We know we cannot understand them, as still less can they understand us, nor can we do much to them on the mental plane, except to make them nervous. Then let us not try to, but mock them a little and let them be a little cross. This is good-natured and sensible, it is much better than trying to invade their world, as some cat lovers do, with the likelihood of ending up, like that poor old female cousin of mine, in a no-man's (and no animal's) land of grievance and pretence. But to be frankly fanciful, to invent stories about cats, to give them human clothing and human feelings, to put words in their mouths, and accompanying the tales we tell of them with bright pictures, there is no harm in this—so long as we do not pretend they are not fancies—no harm and much pleasure.

Yes, these animal fables and fairy stories are full of pleasure. My own favourite of all the cat fairy stories is the one called 'The White Cat'. I forget exactly how it goes, but there was I think the usual youngest of three royal brothers, and this young prince, adventuring in search of treasure beyond gold, finds himself in a great underground candelabra-ed palace. So lofty are these chambers, and so distant their painted walls, the soft lights cannot light them but leave many shadows. The servants in this palace were invisible except for their hands and the Queen of it all was a great white cat, very fine, and finely dressed and bejewelled, and all the lords and ladies who attended her were cats also and wore their rich silks and velvets in fine style, with swords for the gentlemen-cats and high Spanish boots. I remember the great silence of this story, and the strangeness of the hands, the human hands moving in the high air, bringing service to the lordly cats and rich food on golden plates.

This was my favourite story when I was a child. But now I think Grandville stands first with me for cat-fancies, certainly for cat fancies in pictures, he is so mad. This eerie and savage artist, as savage and eerie as Fuseli, is at his best with pussycats. But they are not the pussycats of our present book, indeed they are not. I am thinking of one of Grandville's drawings which Lady Aberconway uses in her *Dictionary of Cat Lovers*, so you may see it there. Well, in this picture a young girl-cat stands in front of some very peculiar cowled chimney-pots (one of them has a human face, all might have). This girl-cat is too gaily dressed, in cheap frills and cheap satin. On one side of her stands a nightgown-clad angel cat with wings. But she does not have an angel face, rather sly she looks, this angel, with a grin and a double chin a madam might have. Yes, there is the debased bridal theme about this cat-picture, as well as the angel theme. I think it is truly depraved. On the other side of the girl cat, and pulling her by one arm, as Madam pulls the other, stands the devil-cat, her dark angel, and I fear it is to him she looks. The devil-cat's eyes stare, his body looks hard beneath his harsh fur, but it is a very tough muscular body, you can see how strong he is. And unfurled for flight against the belching chimney cowls of the dark chimneys are his great bats' wings, leathery and clawed.

Well, you do not often get the English drawing cats like this, they will leave this sort of drawing to Monsieur Grandville. Even our mad English, like the strange cat-mad artist Louis Wain, who while he was residing at the Maudsley Hospital for his madness, drew all the nursing staff and the doctors and psychiatrists in cat forms but true likenesses, are mild and sweet in their fancies, though of rich comicality. Mild and sweet, with occasionally a sly nip, just to show puss he must not get too big for his boots, that is the English cat-comical mood, and it can be a true feeling and not sentimental, though sentimentality is the danger. Cats in art, cats on comic post-cards, cats in stories. Could any of our pretty pussies in this nice book of ours play their part, given a chance, in our favourite cat stories? Yes, certainly they could. They look demure and prim, fixed in a studio portrait mood, but true cats they are and any fanciful dra-matic human being, with a gift for it, could use any one of them, as his own pet cat may often have been used, for any extravagance you like. Pick your Puss-in-Boots from these pages of photographs, your Dick Whittington cat, your Queen White Cat from my favourite fairy story.

And there are the other stories, too, the 'true' stories of cat heroes . . . and cat villains. The only cat villains I can think of are the cats in the witch trials, and this by reason of the devil's choice that he so often appeared to the witches as 'a greate blacke catte', or gave a cat to a witch to be her familiar 'the devil brought her a cat and said she must feed him with a drop of her blood and call the said cat Mamillian'. But witchcraft is too grim a story for here and its rites too cruel for our pampered pets. Yet I remembered the witch legends of history, as when the Scottish witches were accused of attempting the death of the King and Queen on their sea-passage home to Scotland. The witches swam a cat off the coast of North Berwick, having first christened it 'Margaret', they cast it into the sea to drown and thus—they said—raise a storm-wind to sink the King's ship. For this they were convicted and burnt, for the Scots law was crueller than ours and sent witches to the stake, while we only hanged them. But in both countries the poor cat that belonged to the witch, if he was 'apprehended', might also suffer death by burning or hanging.

People in those days did not recognise, to respect, the two worlds —of the Human Creature and the Animal. There was a cock that turned into a hen—and was tried by Canon Law and burnt for it. We have come a little forward from those days, I think, for nowadays any lack of respect we show for the Animal World, such as to attempt an invasion of it in pursuit of understanding, is something we do out of love, that mistaken too-fond love that makes nervous wrecks of our pets. A witch-cat poem I wrote is called 'My Cats'. You can tell they are witch's cats by their names, and by the second line of the first verse, that is a punning spell-line to bring death.

I like to toss him up and down
A heavy cat weighs half a Crown
With a hey do diddle my cat Brown.

I like to pinch him on the sly
When nobody is passing by
With a hey do diddle my cat Fry.

I like to ruffle up his pride
And watch him skip and turn aside
With a hey do diddle my cat Hyde.

Hey Brown and Fry and Hyde my cats
That sit on tombstones for your mats.

There are witches' cats too in another poem I wrote, (and after this I will let the witch cats go, but they haunt my memory, these poor animals, these simple beasts, to have been so taken and used, their animal nature so wronged, and all for mischief of our human minds that will never let well alone). So here come the last of the witches' cats, and here they do not do very much but to step in and set the ghostly scene: (The poem is called 'Great Unaffected Vampires and the Moon':

> *It was a graveyard scene. The crescent moon*
> *Performed a devil's purpose for she shewed*
> *The earth a-heap where smooth it should have lain;*
> *And in and out the tombs great witches' cats*
> *Played tig-a-tag and sang harmoniously.*
> *Beneath the deathly slopes the palings stood*
> *Catching the moonlight on their painted sides,*
> *Beyond, the waters of a mighty lake*
> *Stretching five furlongs at its fullest length*
> *Lay as a looking-glass, framed in a growth*
> *Of leafless willows; all its middle part*
> *Was open to the sky, and there I saw*
> *Embosomed in the lake together lie*
> *Great unaffected vampires and the moon.*
> *A Christian crescent never would have lent*
> *Unchristian monsters such close company*
> *And so I say she was no heavenly light*
> *But devil's in that business manifest*
> *And as the vampires seemed quite unaware*
> *I thought she'd lost her soul for nothing lying there.*

This poem, for all that the cats play so small a part in it, brings to mind another favourite aspect of cat-fancying—I mean, the cat in ghost stories. A writer who used them much in this way, and always with the deepest respect and affection—perhaps too much respect, for are they quite as 'grand' as he paints them?—was Algernon Blackwood. There is one story of his one cannot forget, not only because it is in all the anthologies, but for its quality. It is called 'Ancient Sorceries'. Do you remember . . . ? But of course, now I come to think of it, this, too, is a witch story. Poor pussycats, how linked they are with the black arts, so plump and peaceful by day, so feared by night, crossing the moon on their perilous broomsticks. In this story of Blackwood's there is a young man of French descent who is travelling in France on holiday. Suddenly the train he is on pulls up at a little station and he feels he must get down at this station. The inn he goes to is sleepy and comfortable, the proprietress is also sleepy and comfortable, a large fat lady who moves silently on little fat feet. Everybody in this inn treads silently, and all the people in the town are like this too, sleepy, heavy and treading softly. After a few days the young man begins to wonder; and at night, waking to look out over the ancient roof-tops, he wonders still more. For there is a sense of soft movement in the air, of doors opening softly, of soft thuds as soft bodies drop to the ground from wall or window; and he sees the shadows moving too. It was the shadow of a human being that dropped from the wall, but the shadow moved on the ground as a cat runs, and now it was not a human being but a cat. So in the end of course the young man is invited by the cat-girl, who is the plump inn owner's daughter and serves by day in the inn, to join 'the dance' that is the witch's sabbath. For this old French town is a mediaeval witch-town and bears the past alive within it. Being highminded, as most ghost-writers are, Blackwood makes the young man refuse the invitation and so come safe off with his soul, which had been for a moment much imperilled.

In other stories Blackwood keeps his cats on the side of the angels, the good angels that is. They serve then to give warning of evil ghosts coming up on the night hour in some house of evil history. Blackwood thought, as many people think to this day, that cats have an especial awareness of ghosts and ghostliness, even more so than dogs, who are allowed all the same I believe, by people who are informed in such matters, some disturbance of their hackles when ghosts walk.

I have come a long way from the pages of cat photographs you will soon be turning to, or perhaps have already turned to, as introductions are written to be skipped. But if you look at these pretty cats and think I have wronged them, or look at them and think they do not tell the whole cat-story and wish some other sort of cat was there, remember—the cat for all its prettiness or ugliness, high bred under human discipline or got by chance, is a blank page for you to write what you like on. Remember too that what you write throws no light on puss but only on yourself, and so be happy and leave him to his darkness. As I was content to do, I hope, in the poem I called 'My Cat Major':

Major is a fine cat
What is he at?
He hunts birds in the hydrangea
And in the tree
Major was ever a ranger
He ranges where no one can see.

Sometimes he goes up to the attic
With a hooped back
His paws hit the iron rungs
Of the ladder in a quick kick
How can this be done?
It is a knack.

Oh Major is a fine cat
He walks cleverly
And what is he at, my fine cat?
No one can see.

I will finish with the Story of a Good Cat. This was the cat who came to the cruel cold prison in which Richard III had cast Sir Henry Wyatt when young. Because of his Lancastrian sympathies Henry had already been imprisoned several times, and even put to the torture. The cat saved his life by drawing pigeons into the cell which the gaoler agreed to cook and dress for the poor prisoner, though for fear of his own life he dared not by other means increase his diet. There is a picture of Sir Henry as an old man sitting in a portrait with the prison cell for background and the cat, a peculiar sad-looking little cat, drawing a pigeon through the prison bars. Underneath is written, but so faintly it is difficult to read, 'This Knight with hunger, cold and care neere starved, pyncht, pynde away, The sillie Beast did feede, heat, cheere with dyett, warmth and playe'.

It is an amiable part of human nature, that we should love our animals; it is even better to love them to the point of folly, than not to love them at all.

1959

SYLER'S GREEN:

a return journey

Syler's Green, Syler's Green, dear suburb of my infancy. How well I remember the first time I ever saw Syler's Green. It was on a September afternoon, many many years ago. I was four years old. My mother and my Aunt, my sister and myself, had just arrived from Hull, in Yorkshire. My Aunt, who had gone on ahead, had taken this house in Syler's Green as a short resting place until we could find something that suited us better. My sister aged six and myself thought at once it was a very beautiful house and a beautiful garden.

We went round the corner to our Landlord's shop—he was a plumber—to make some arrangements and to get me weighed. I was always being weighed for some reason or another. He had some enormous weighing machines, the sort they use for luggage.

'You are a fine package,' said Mr Blom our landlord.

'Ah came on a train and then on a tram,' I said with a fine strong Yorkshire accent.

'Why you're a furriner,' said Mr Blom, 'you're a foreign package, yes you are.' And he lifted me down from the scales.

That is my first memory of Syler's Green. Needless to say we children were right about the house. Although our cautious elders would at first only sign a lease for six months, we stayed in that house for a great many years, and in the end we bought it from Mr Blom.

The next thing I remember is the woods. Syler's Green in those days was more of a country place than a suburb. And just behind our house, on the other side of the railway cutting, were these vast mysterious dark and wonderful woods. They were privately owned and trespassers were forbidden. This of course made it all the more exciting.

You are never to cross the railway line, children, now Pearl (this to my sister) you are to see that Patsy (that was me) never crosses the railway line.

We promised that we would never do such a thing. But we found a large pipe that ran under the railway line, and we used to crawl through that and run up the high grass slopes of the cutting. At the top was the beginning of the wood, and this part of the woods we used to call Paradise.

Now the whole of Syler's Green when we first went there was a very beautiful place to live in, especially for young children. There were fields to play in and shady country lanes, and farmhouses with their cows and the pigs and there was a toll gate, with its barred gate a-swing and a little house at the side of it for the toll-keeper. It was a long time ago you know, and a ripe September time with the autumn sunshine in the air and the rich smell of acorns and damp mould and the michaelmas daisies, especially there was the smell of the large rich michaelmas daisies that grew in the churchyard. Of course it wasn't always September or always sunny but that is how one is apt to remember past times, it is always a sunny day. This sunny time of a happy childhood seems like a golden age, a time untouched by war, a dream of innocent quiet happenings, a dream in which people go quietly about their blameless business, bringing their garden marrows to the Harvest Festival, believing in God, believing in peace, believing in Progress (which of course is always progress in the right direction), believing in the catechism and even believing in that item of the catechism which is so frequently misquoted by the careless and indignant . . . 'to do my duty in that state of life to which it shall please God to call me' (and not 'to which it has pleased God to call me'); believing also that the horrible things of life always happen abroad or to the undeserving poor and that no good comes from brooding upon them—indeed it is not wholesome to do so—although an interest in one's neighbours' affairs is only natural. And indeed how can society be wholesome if everything is not above board?—believing in fact a great deal of nonsense along with the sense.

And much we children cared about all this, indeed we never gave it a thought. We were far too busy with our wonderful deep exciting devilish woods, for devilish they seemed as we came into them from the bright sunshine and dived into their dark shadows, devilish and devilishly exciting. Paradise as I have explained was that part of the wood which lay just behind the railway cutting, an open pleasant place it was with a little stream, all open and sunny as the day itself. But behind that again lay the dark wood, with the trees growing close together, the dark holly trees, the tall beeches and the mighty oak trees. And there too was the Keeper's cottage, and it was the Keeper's business to keep us out. This Keeper was our ogre, our dragon and our enemy. We devoted a great deal of our time to outwitting the creature. He would walk silently with a woodman's-red-

Indian's silence upon the twigs through the undergrowth, and he was always accompanied by a large black curly-coated retriever dog, who answered to the name of Caesar.

The grandest of all the paths in this wood, Longmans path, was a really beautiful path—but dangerous, for it led straight to the Keeper's cottage. It had almost everything that a path through a wood should have, it went up and down, it ran through bracken, it was crossed by a stream that was wide enough to make a running jump necessary—and even then one might if one's legs were short and one's take-off careless, land in the shallow water and go well up to the knees in black loamish mud. It also had a witches' pool, about halfway down the path and still just far enough from the Cottage to make a picnic safe, well fairly safe. Our witches' pool was a pool of water fed by a spring, it had a beach of fine white sand and it was overhung by a very old and knobbly oak tree, whose roots, half exposed, struck down into the water. The sandy banks harboured hosts of rabbits and their holes made a handy cache for our various treasure. I remember I once left a copy of my Aunt's favourite book —Francis Younghusband's *The Relief of Chitral*—in one of these holes, and never recovered it. Perhaps the rabbits devoured it with as much enjoyment as my Aunt.

Yes, in those early days Syler's Green was more of a country place than a suburb, but already the fields were beginning to be broken up and the woods parcelled out and the trees marked for cutting down.

The railway station at Syler's Green bears the date of the Franco-Prussian war—1870, and has the endearing style of its period, the wood-lace frill to the canopy over the platform, the Swiss Chalet appearance of the very sooty-brick station, and the black brick walls thrusting back against the grass banks and made bright by the coloured advertisements pasted on them. I remember these advertisements too.

'The Pickwick, the Owl and the Waverley pen, they came as a boon and a blessing to men,' and that early Jeyes Fluid advertisement. There is the nurse, there is something one feels of Lady Macbeth in her character, she is slowly washing her hands. Her eyes are staring straight ahead. She knows that Jeyes Fluid will not wash out that stain, but it will perhaps disinfect it a little. There was also a very handsome soldier, or so I thought him—but a little caddish perhaps, a thought too well appointed?—who with his tight laced body, his devilish cap and his black swirling moustache, advertised

Dandy Fifth tobacco. But these advertisements, with the date on the station bridge, were anachronisms and had really no business in the Syler's Green of my childhood, that was already thrusting ahead and bustling along to the first World War.

There were two or three large estates in Syler's Green which after a while were sold. One of them is especially vivid in my memory. This estate belonged to a Greek banking family. The Greek family had children of our age, and every year in the summer they used to give an enormous hay party. I remember wearing a stiffly starched white sailor suit and going to this party with my sister and the little boy from next door, who was, we thought, rather a muff. Alan did not live next door, he only stayed there sometimes with his aunts. These two ladies, and their companion lady, were neighbours of ours all through my childhood. The two property-owning ladies were called Jessie and Emmeline, and their companion was always called 'Miss Baby'. They had a stone statue of a Roman boy in their garden, they also had a fat white fox terrier dog called Beano. Miss Baby used to do a lot of work for Foreign Missions. She asked us once if we would let her have any old gym stockings that we did not want. 'What do you want them for?' I asked her. 'For the 'eathen,' she said. She used to cut them down and make them into jersey suits.

Miss Baby was a cheerful happy person in spite of 'the 'eathen' and the fact that she had once been to a bonesetter who had so mishandled her poor frame that she could now walk only with the aid of the furniture, from piece to piece of which she would fling herself in search of Miss Jessie's spectacles or a cup of morning milk for the employers, but Miss Emmeline was full of doom. It was from Miss Emmeline that we first learnt about the White Slave Traffic. Our mother was rather annoyed when we asked her about this—though Miss Emmeline like a true prophetess of gloom had been far from explicit. 'I have told you, Patsy,' said Mama, 'that you are never to speak to strangers in the street or to accept sweets from them, so run along and do as I tell you and don't bother your head about the White Slave Traffic.' But Miss Emmeline had fired our imaginations.

'If a lady comes up to you in a closed cab and leans out of the window and asks you to get in, don't you have anything to do with her,' said Miss Emmeline. And then she seized my hand and pulled me close up to her (I can smell her old-lady smell now, the lavender and mothball, the dusty velvet ribbon, the menthol lozenges she used to suck and sometimes the faint smell of the old dog Beano clinging about her skirts). 'It is the White Slave Traffic,' she said. And one day she said again, 'If a lady comes up to you and tells you that your dear mama is lying in a faint on the pavement round the corner, don't you believe her, don't have anything to do with her, do not go with her into the cab. It is the White Slave Traffic.'

It seemed that if you yielded to the blandishments of this lady in a cab you would become a White Slave. And what would happen to you then? Ah, that we did not know.

Now of course children always play what they hear. And just as, during the recent war, you might see the children at their war-games (for instance the little boy who lived opposite us used to scoot round on his scooter-cycle crying out, 'Coming in to attack, Coming in to attack') so we, in those far off days of our childhood, used to play this game of the White Slave Traffic that was so very much a game of *that* period, for all the apparently sunny innocent and pastoral nature of our suburb. For might not the Lady of the Cab come bowling along those country lanes at any sunny moment, herself more fearful grisly and truly sinister by reason of the sunshine that shone on the black boxlike vehicle in which she travelled and the black satin and jet in which she would no doubt be clad, and the befeathered black hat and veil which would conceal her pale and wicked face? Our imaginations in fact, fired by Miss Emmeline's stories, were very far from boggling at such a proposition, and we used to play the game with great gusto, trundling our dolls downstairs on teatrays—they were the white slaves—and bundling them off in the dolls' pram—the 'cab' of course—to some rather shadowy destination. I remember for a long time I used to think that the waxwork child-models displaying clothes in the drapers' shop windows were really the white slave children who had been changed into statues, and that here indeed might truly be discerned—The Sinister Hand of the White Slavers.

As a matter of fact I was rather fond of Miss Emmeline and I think she was rather fond of me because she often used to take me up to the cemetery for an afternoon's walk. The memory of these graveyard excursions fired me later on to write a very solemn poem indeed, which, for a reason I do not remember, I called 'Breughel'.

> *The ages blaspheme*
> *The people are weak*
> *As in a dream*
> *They evilly speak.*

Their words in a clatter
Of meaningless sound
Without form or matter
Echo around.

The people oh Lord
Are sinful and sad
Prenatally biassed
Grow worser born bad

They sicken oh Lord
They have no strength in them
Oh rouse up my God
And against their will win them.

Must thy lambs to the slaughter
Delivered be
With each son and daughter
Irrevocably?

From tower and steeple
Ring out funeral bells
Oh Lord save thy people
They have no help else.

At the age of five one must of course go to school. And now, if you will please picture my schooldays against a background of new houses sprouting up, of muddy roads, with the drain pipes being laid, of tall brick stacks and curb-stones at crazy angles at the road-sides, I will tell you about the early suburban schooldays. Our schooldays were directed by a most unusual woman. She was a Quaker lady and had a real devotion to teaching. She had gathered several of her relations around her and they had pooled their money and set up this school. She was a very staunch lady and believed in herself and her gifts. She was a very outspoken woman too and at the beginning of the first World War made herself quite unpopular because she thought that a certain poem that was in favour at that time was nonsense. Do you remember that poem I wonder? 'You have boasted the day, You have toasted the day, and now the day has come.' It was called 'The Day' and was aimed at the Kaiser. It was written by a railway porter.

But in the Kindergarten all was dash and gaiety, we had no time for the Kaiser. We were hearing about the Transvaal and the covered wagons and moreover we were making the covered wagons out of matchboxes, with linen buttons for wheels, and cartridge paper, cut to size, for the canopy.

When I was promoted to the Transition Class, life seemed even more wonderful. We were told the story of Beowulf and how he tore off Grendel's arm in the depths of the lake (and this tale we used of course to play later in the woods and by the great lake in Scapelands Park); and above all we were learning in our geography lessons about the tropics. Oh those tropics, how much I loved them (although I had and still have a horror of snakes). But our form-mistress who combined geography with painting—and subsequently left us for ever to study Egyptology under Flinders Petrie and go out digging with him to Egypt—had a real gift for bringing the jungle home to a young child of tender years.

'Now children,' she would say, 'have you got any large hat boxes or dress boxes at home?'

Yes, yes, our mamas had plenty of such boxes.

'Then bring them along with you tomorrow, and bring some moss to lay flat in the bottom of the box and then we can begin with our jungle scene.'

The next day we would set to work in earnest. With rich indigoes and blues and ochres and greens we would slosh the inside of the box lid until it looked, to our inspired imagination (inspired by our mistress's description), exactly like the jungle and the tropical forest scene. And in this jungle would crawl and fly and climb and jabber and whine and shriek all the animals, birds and reptiles we had heard about, and seen in visits to the zoo, and seen in the bright pictures our mistress used to hand round.

This school was extremely strong in history, literature and geography but I fear it was an unorthodox education and today would be frowned upon. Indeed today such a school could not exist. For the headmistress and her assistants were none of them qualified in the academic sense to teach anything. But we learned a lot from them for all that.

We also had a very good selection of poems to read from in our literature lessons. I do not know who made this anthology but it had a great many poems in it that we liked to recite. There was

'The Pibroch of Doneil Dhu'.

> *Pibroch of Doneil Dhu*
> *Pibroch of Doneil*
> *Wake thy wild voice anew*
> *Summon Clan Conneil*
> *Come as the winds come when forests are rended*
> *Come as the waves come when navies are stranded*
> *Faster come faster come, faster and faster,*
> *Chief, vassal, page and groom, tenant and master.*

Needless to say we learnt the whole of 'Horatius' by heart and took great pleasure in those lolloping lines.

> *But nearer fast and nearer*
> *Doth the red whirlwind come*
> *And louder still and still more loud*
> *From underneath the rolling cloud*
> *Is heard the trumpet's war note proud,*
> *The trampling and the hum*
> *And plainly and more plainly*
> *Now through the gloom appears*
> *Far to the left and far to the right*
> *In broken gleams of dark blue light*
> *The long array of helmets bright*
> *The long array of spears.*

I am quoting without the book as I remember it, so it may be wrong. We also liked

> *North looked the Dictator north looked he long and hard*
> *Then spoke to Caius Cossus the captain of the guard*
> *Caius of all the Romans thou hast the keenest sight*
> *Say what from yonder cloud of dust*
> *Comes from the Latian right?*

Then Caius says those wonderful lines ending up with:

> *I see the dark blue charger and far before the best*
> *I see the dark blue charger I see the purple vest*

72

> *I see the something something that shines far off like flame*
> *Thus over rides Mamilius Prince of the Latian name.*

How grand it sounded, 'Prince of the Latian name.'

But our headmistress was rather against war and used to try and interest us in anti-war poems like Longfellow's poem.

> *This is the arsenal from floor to ceiling*
> *Like a huge organ rise the burnished arms*
> *But from their silent pipes no anthem stealing*
> *Wakens the village with strange alarms*
> *Oh what a sound shall rise how dim and dreary*
> *When the Death Angel touches those swift keys*
> *What loud lament and dismal miserere*
> *Will mingle with their awful symphonies.*

But this one was pretty war-like too, we thought, although it was saying how awful it all was, so we liked this poem and we liked the lines that come later on.

> *And Aztec priests upon their Teocallis*
> *Beat the wild wardrums made of serpents' skins.*

And how we liked that other poem of Macaulay's, at least how I liked it, but if I have no right to say what the other children liked, at least I can say that we all seemed to enjoy saying this poem out loud:

> *The still glassy lake that sleeps*
> *Beneath Aricia's trees*
> *Those trees in whose dim shadow*
> *The ghastly priest doth reign*

and then the final appalling lines, heavy and haunting with their secret meaning:

> *The priest who slew the slayer,*
> *And shall himself be slain.*

Our headmistress believed in discipline and she had a high—some people might think a rather simple—moral code. But there was a fine

73

touch of melodrama about one of our headmistress's favourite poems which went something like this:

> *Tomorrow she told her conscience*
> *Tomorrow I mean to be good*
> *Tomorrow I'll do as I ought*
> *Tomorrow I'll think as I should*
> *Tomorrow I'll conquer the passions*
> *That keep me from heaven away*
> *But ever her conscience whispered*
> *One word and one only, Today.*
> *Tomorrow tomorrow tomorrow*
> *And thus through the years it went on*
> *Tomorrow tomorrow tomorrow*
> *Till youth like a shadow was gone*
> *Till age and her passions had written*
> *The message of fate on her brow*
> *And forth from the shadows came Death*
> *With the terrible syllable, Now.*

Yes, we liked that one, and our headmistress, like other more professional readers of verse, did not pull her punches when it was a matter of 'expression', that 'Now' fairly shot us away.

We were supposed to be ladylike at our high school. Our headmistress used to talk about 'my girls', especially when 'my girls' had been guilty of some misdemeanour, this, we were told, was not like 'my girls'. We were in fact to hold ourselves distinct from the less fortunate infants who attended the County School, or those even more benighted who picked up their three R's at the Board School. As a part of this separateness, we never wore common gym tunics, no we wore neat navy blue dresses with green buttons and belts and white collars, and for drill we wore navy blue kilts and jerseys with pale Cambridge blue collars and sashes. At drill one of our favourite exercises was the rowing boat exercise. We used to sit on the brightly polished floor and row ourselves backwards and forwards, and all the time we were singing our beautiful rowing song:

> *Here we float*
> *In our golden boat*
> *Far away far away*

Here we float in our golden boat
Far away
See how we splash
And water dash
While in the air
The sun shines fair
Singing of birds
And lowing herds
Far away.

More serious but equally popular were the hymns we sang at
morning prayers. These we were allowed to choose for ourselves. I
remember my first kindergarten hymn, the first I ever remember
singing, I remember it word for word, and I remember the tune,
though I cannot have been more than five when we sang it:

Great big wonderful beautiful world
With the wonderful waters around you curled
And the wonderful grass upon your breast
World you are wonderfully beautifully dressed.

But with added years our sense of responsibility grew. A not unfa-
vourite hymn contained some serious matter, although the tune was
as gay as a jig:

Opportunities of little passed unheeded by-y-y
Make one sad gigantic failure for Eternity

Phew, that was no laughing matter.

As you see, in those early days at Syler's Green, we were a small
community with common interests, and a little harmless snobbery to
give zest to life.

I think it was a fairly harmless snobbery, for my family as a matter
of fact was always hard up and we lived in a small house and never
had a maid, but it never seemed to make any difference, although I
suppose it would be better for the drama of the thing, if I could tell
you how persecuted I was and how my schoolmates held off from me
for that reason, but this was not the case.

I had one particular crony, a half-French child of my own age, who
was then about ten. She was called Nica. I am afraid Nica and I did
not always behave like our headmistress's 'girls' for our chief delight

was to climb a wall and crawl along the top of it past other people's gardens right down the whole length of the road. In this way we had a wonderful view of a variety of gardens and we had also the difficulty of dodging under the overhanging trees and shrubs, and of course of 'not being seen'. To screw up our courage against the hazards of this journey, we used to sing under our breath a song that was a particular favourite of Nica and myself, and I may say with this song we used to drive our parents pretty mad; it went like this:

> *Flee-va-la flee-va-la flee-va-la flee*
> *The animals went in two by two*
> *Flee-va-la compagnie*
> *Flee-va-la flee-va-la flee-va-la flee*
> *The elephant and the kangaroo*
> *Flee-va-la compagnie*

And so on.

And it was about this time I think that I wrote my first poem about which I had a very high opinion. This opinion was not shared by my aunt who I am afraid, along with certain other of my activities, thought it 'unnecessary'. My poem went like this:

> *Spanky Wanky had a sister*
> *He said, I'm sure a black man kissed her*
> *For she's got a spot just here*
> *Twas a beauty spot my dear*
> *And it looks most awfully quaint*
> *Like a blob of jet black paint*
> *But when he told his sister that*
> *She threw at him her gorgeous hat*
> *And with airs that made her swanky*
> *Said, I hate you Spanky Wanky*

The civic and cultural sense of our suburb developed early. As quite a young child I was taken to the Literary Society's lectures and lantern shows. I remember one fascinating lecture on the Moon; it was given by an old clergyman called Dr Iremonger. He had a slight impediment in his speech, but such was his enthusiasm for the moon and so remarkable were his illustrating slides, that he was one of the Society's most popular figures and was often required to repeat his lecture.

We also had a great many dramatic societies, and of course tennis clubs, croquet clubs, Shakespeare Societies, swimming clubs, rambling clubs; politics also were not forgotten, we had the Labour Party, the Liberal Party, the Primrose League and later the Communist Party.

But there is no doubt about it, our early life in Syler's Green centred naturally enough in the church and the school. Church was exciting, there always seemed to be something going on. The Reverend D'Aurevilly Cole was a scholarly rather eccentric but very loving person. But I believe he was something of a trial to the church council because he was so very absentminded. I remember my aunt coming home one day in quite a furious mood. 'He really is a trying individual,' she said, 'he is really very trying. All the time Mr Harbottle was giving the estimate for the new cassocks and for the heating plant that is to be installed in the new hall he was laughing quietly to himself. The doctor,' she said, 'who was sitting beside him on the platform, kept nudging him to stop laughing, and the vicar said, "What's the matter Blane, why do you keep nudging me?" Everybody could hear what was going on, it was most unfortunate. So then the doctor explained that Mr Harbottle was rather hurt that the vicar was laughing, and the vicar said "Oh I wasn't laughing at you, Harbottle, it was just something that I was thinking about, just something that was passing through my mind." '

But he was a very kind man and sent an invalid girl who used to go to church to Italy for a holiday with her brother, and as they had hardly a penny to bless themselves with, he paid for the whole holiday himself.

We used to be taken to church in the morning to attend Matins, and I always used to decide before we went to church which hymn I was going to sing. This was generally 'Once in Royal David's City', and I sang it, and it did not matter at all that everybody else was singing something different.

My sister and I used specially to enjoy the festivals when the great banners were carried round the church. There was one that had been given to the Scouts' Company by the wife of the old Scoutmaster who had died. He was called Edwin Alton Crumbles, and his name was printed in full on the back of the banner and when it went round and back again to the altar my sister and I used to chant, under our breath I hope, 'Edwin Alton amen, Pray for me and all men.' In the afternoon we used to go to Sunday School, and here we sat in small classes in the church hall, and I can still smell the smell of the scrubbed flooring and the rather dusty smell of the hassocks and the great red velvet curtains, that hung down upon the raised stage at the end of the hall. Just as I can still smell the quite different pine wood, leather and brick smell of the church itself. I was once given a copy of *King Solomon's Mines* as a prize but rather also I think, since it was given to me in class by Miss Frond our Sunday School mistress, to keep me quiet. I remember that I borrowed her fountain pen and wrote on the paper cover at the back of the book my name and address: 'Syler's Green, North London, England, North West Europe, The World.' I then sat down on the book and blotted the ink address on my white muslin dress. But that address is rather true in a way, for I do not think you can know anything very much about the world unless you are fortunate enough to know something about that address as you read it backwards.

It is very fortunate to grow up as we grew up, in a quiet place that has the appearance of going on being the same really for ever, instead of growing up to wander homeless, to be driven homeless from place to place, and to know hunger and to know what it is to have no home and no parents, but to take as matters of course that ruins are your home and that persons unrelated to you, remote if friendly, and in uniform, are to direct your lives; as now is the commonplace of Europe.

Our suburb nowadays is very large and very bustling, but the bones of the older situation are still there. I suppose in the social sense it has 'gone down'. It was once a place for bankers, stock-brokers, doctors and naval officers; but now the larger houses are let off in flats, sometimes they are just as they were but several families live in the houses; now there are no such things as lantern slides, there are two large cinemas instead, and there are dancing halls and I believe, yes it is true, there is even a fried fish shop. But the people are bustling and happy as ever, and one thing they seem to me to have in quite extraordinary abundance, and that is babies. The busy shopping streets are crowded with prams and of course dogs. Oh those dogs, it is about the dogs of Syler's Green that I wrote my poem called the Dogs of England.

O happy dogs of England
Bark well as bark you may

If you lived anywhere else
You would not be so gay.

O happy dogs of England
Bark well at errand boys
If you lived anywhere else
You would not be allowed to make such an infernal noise.

But no doubt the dogs of Syler's Green are excited by the fine air of these parts, for ours is a very high-lying healthy suburb and at the top of our hill they say with pride that we are the highest spot between where we are and the Ural Mountains. Of course if you happened to look west instead of east it would be a different story because of the Welsh Mountains.

And now can you guess which suburb it is? Well, I dare say you can. And for my part when I climb that hill again I shall look firmly towards the east and I shall think about being the highest spot between where I am and the Ural Mountains, and I shall say that we are not only this healthy suburb where babies may flourish but we are also to be *envied* and *congratulated* because we have our rich community life and are not existing in a bored box-like existence that is what people think of suburb life, and that all this is due to the fact that by the mercy of heaven we are not one of those new suburbs but have our roots in the old country place that was there before the houses grew up, and that because we have been kind to the country and have kept the beautiful oak trees and the wide estates in which they grow, that we have kept them for wide spacious parks, so because we have done this the country has also been kind to us. For we might have sold them to make more money and cut down the century old fine trees and filled in the vast deep lake that is in Scapeland's park and on which when the frost is hard we wheel out the babies and skate and slide, we might have done away with all this and built more roads and more houses. And this we did not do.

But do you know sometimes in a black-dog moment I wish that the great trees that I remember in my childhood and the even greater trees and the dense forests that were in these parts long long before I was born, would come again, thrusting up their great bodies and throwing up the paving stones, the tarmac roads and the neat rows of pleasant houses, and that once again it could be all forest land and dangerous thickets where only the wolves and the wild boars had their homes. And there in the green depths of Scapelands Lake lay the body of Grendel with her arm torn off. She is mourning her son, the Monster, slain by Beowulf.

Those gentle woods of my remembered childhood have had a serious effect upon me, make no doubt about it. Half wishing for them half fearing them, it is like the poem I wrote about them:

> *The wood was rather old and dark*
> *The witch was very ugly*
> *And if it hadn't been for father*
> *Walking there so smugly*
> *I never should have followed*
> *The beckoning of her finger.*
> *Ah me how long ago it was*
> *And still I linger*
> *Under the ever-interlacing beeches*
> *Over a carpet of moss*
> *I lift my hand but it never reaches*
> *To where the breezes toss*
> *The sun-kissed leaves above.*
> *The sun?*
> *Beware.*
> *The sun never comes here.*
> *Round about and round I go*
> *Up and down and to and fro*
> *The woodlouse hops upon the tree*
> *Or should do but I really cannot see.*
> *Happy fellow. Why can't I be*
> *Happy as he?*
> *The wood grows darker every day*
> *It's not a bad place in a way*
> *But I lost the way*
> *Last Tuesday*
> *Did I love father, mother, home?*
> *Not very much; but now they're gone*
> *I think of them with kindly toleration*
> *Bred inevitably of separation.*
> *Really if I could find some food*
> *I should be happy enough in this wood*
> *But darker days and hungrier I must spend*
> *Till hunger and darkness make an end.*

Only those who have the luxury of a beautiful kindly bustling suburb that is theirs for the taking and of that 'customary domestic kindness' that De Quincey speaks of, can indulge themselves in these antagonistic forest-thoughts. And of course we may observe that only these ever do. And was there ever such a suburb as Syler's Green for the promotion of briskness, shrewdness, neighbourliness, the civic sense and *No Nonsense?* There was not. And so with this sniff of regional pride and smug self-righteousness I will say goodbye to the happy place of my childhood. And where is it, where is it?

> *Syler's Green,*
> *Syler's Green,*
> *Listener, have you ever seen*
> *Syler's Green?*

1947

A LONDON SUBURB

I like old suburbs that have grown from country places. They stand ten miles from London and ten miles from a countryside that is still unspoilt because the train service is so bad. The railway station is of the Swiss chalet pattern and has a wooden lace canopy over the platforms. It once took a prize for the beauty of its flower beds.

The shops in the High Street of the suburb are rather ugly. There are a great many shoe shops and sweet shops and hair-dressers' shops and drapers. There is an undertaker's shop with a china angel standing on a mauve table cloth. In the office of this shop the undertaker has a blotting pad of mauve blotting paper mounted on a piece of artificial green turf. The pub in the High Street has Georgian bay windows and a Tudor doorway; the turrets on the little tower are from chateau-panto-land; the flagpost mounts a golden fox. There is a Ritz Café where the ladies of the suburb gather for morning coffee and there are two cinemas, the Palmadium and the Green Hall.

Round the corner from the High Street are the old houses and the village pound and the old pubs and the old church. The old houses have names like Hope House and The Wilderness. They are not very convenient to live in and are frequently let as offices, or they may be museums holding pictures, records and the bones of old animals who roamed in past days.

In the straight streets planted with trees and fringed with grass plots stand the modern houses where the families live. These houses have quite different sorts of names from the old houses. The modern names are written on the garden gates or slung in fretwork over the porch. The Cedars, Cumfy, Dunromin, the more original Dunsekin, Trottalong. There is the house that is called Home Rails (a happy investment, fortune-founding?). There is Deo Data for the learned, Villa Roma for the travelled, Portarlington Lodge for the socially ambitious. Ella, Basil and Ronald live at Elbasron. There is also Elasrofton which is 'not for sale' written backwards.

The place names on the way to the city where the fathers go daily to earn their living are countrified—the mysterious Cockfosters, Green Lanes, Wood Green, Turnpike Lane. Coming nearer to the city there is Manor Park. And what is that curious building, an exact copy of Stirling Castle, that stands to the left of the bus route? It is the Waterworks.

In the high-lying outer northern suburb the wind blows fresh and keen, the clouds drive swiftly before it, the pink almond blossom blows away. When the sun is going down in stormy red clouds the whole suburb is pink, the light is a pink light; the high brick walls that are still left standing where once the old estates were hold the pink light and throw it back. The laburnum flowers on the pavement trees are yellow, so there is this pink and yellow colour, and the blue-grey of the roadway, that are special to this suburb. The slim stems of the garden trees make a dark line against the delicate colours. There is also the mauve and white lilac.

Many years ago the suburb was a great woodland country-side, it was a forest preserve and across its wooded acres tore the wild boar and the red deer, and after them came the mounted nobility who made sure by the ferocity of the game laws that none but they should hunt.

In Scapelands Hall at the beginning of the century (that is now Scapelands Park and a fine public place) lived the great Lord Cattermole, and he rode with his little son and put his horse Midas at the moat that lies round the Vanbrugh House that is now a Hospital of Recovery: he cleared the moat, but his son did not; the son fell with his head against the brick moat and ever afterwards he was weak in his head. They moved away before the wars came.

Behind the thick laurel bushes which border the drive that leads to Hope House there lay one day the body of Thessapopoulos Thereidi the international financier, the great Greek banker. The hand of the assassin had struck him down as he came one night late from his carriage. The body lay three days before it was found by his cook-housekeeper. Hope House is now the Offices of the Metropolitan Water Board, and the coach house that adjoins the main building is in the hands of the agent for the Recovery of Income Tax.

Suburban fast life centres in the club-houses above the shops and cinemas, and in the funfairs at the London side of the suburb which are thought to be rather 'common'. These funfairs, they say, 'let the suburb down'. The fast ladies wear plaid slacks and have long yellow-dyed hair and the cigarette is firmly stuck to the lower lip as they trundle out the babies and the beer bottles. The pubs where these ladies are also to be found have names that are older than the suburb—The Fox, The Dog and Duck, The Woodman, The Pike, The Cattermole Arms, The Cock, The Serpent of Hadley, The World's End.

There is much going on in the suburb for those who seek company. There is the Shakespeare Reading Society, the Allotment Growers' Club; there is a Players' Society in connection with the local theatre; there are the amateur dramatic societies (that are such a delicious hotbed of the emotions—chagrin, display, the managerial mind; pleasure in becoming for one evening a spiv or a lord; ingenuity, competition, meeting young men). There are also the games clubs and the political clubs—tennis, golf, cycling; conservative, labour, communist. There is skating on the indoor rinks, and when the frost is hard, skating too on the great lake in Scapelands Park. There is also riding on the spavined hack or, for those who like danger, on the 'chaser whose temper is as vile as his price was low. The anglers who fish the inshore waters of Scapelands Lake have also their club, but theirs is a silent fellowship. Even the young boys fish silently, but sometimes a bite will stir them to words—'Hang on, man'.

The most beautiful place in the suburb is Scapelands Park, especially when the weather is wild and there is nobody about except the anglers. When the wind blows east and ruffles the water of the lake, driving the rain before it, the Egyptian geese rise with a squawk, and the rhododendron trees, shaken by the gusts, drip the raindrops from the blades of their green-black leaves. The empty park, in the winter rain, has a staunch and inviolate melancholy that is refreshing. For are not sometimes the brightness and busyness of suburbs, the common life and the chatter, the kiddy-cars on the pavements and the dogs, intolerable?

Christianity in the suburb is cheerful. The church is a centre of social activity and those who go to church need never be lonely. The stained glass windows in the church, which are of the Burne-Jones school and not very good, have been subscribed for by loving relations to commemorate the friends of the church and the young men killed in the wars. There is cheerfulness and courage in the church community, and modesty in doing good.

Now turn for a moment to the inner suburbs of London, those places of gloom and fancy. The names of these suburbs, although at first sight they seem pretty enough, have dank undertones—Mildmay Park, Noel Park, Northumberland Park. They suggest November fog and sooty chimneys and visions of decay. Behind heavy rep curtains, and an inner curtain of yellowing net, a parrot swings in his cage. At the corner of the street is a tin chapel with a crimson roof.

The advertisements at the tobacconist's are enamelled in royal blue and yellow on iron sheets. A canal moves sluggishly between mildewed stone bannisters. There is always a fog in the cemetery. London has captured these places, and the cheerfulness of their pubs and music-halls is a London cheerfulness; they must not be counted as suburbs.

The true suburb is the outer suburb and it is of the outer suburb that I am writing.

In Scapelands Park of a fine Sunday afternoon you may snuff the quick-witted high-lying life of a true suburban community. Here the young girls swing arm in arm round the path that borders the still lake-water. As they swing past the boys who are coming to meet them, the girls cry out, to the boys, 'Okey-doke, phone me'. In the deck chair beside the pavilion the old gentleman is talking to his friend, 'It is my birthday today and my wife would have me adorned. She put this suit on me' (he points to the flower in his buttonhole) 'and sent to have me adorned.' By the cage of budgerigars sits the ageing Miss Cattermole, who is rather mad. She wears a pink scarf 'to keep the evil spirits away'. She says the vicar is plotting to kill her.

If you sit by the brink of the lake you may catch the flash of a large fish as he passes at depth; or you may lie on your back and look up at the summer leaves of the tall poplar tree that are always moving. They are like fish-scales of pale green. They make a clattering sound as they turn on the wind. The bad-tempered swan hisses at the barking dog, the swan's neck is caked with mud and has a lump on it. At the corner by the woods the water of the lake is very dark, it is forty feet deep, and speaks again of the past, for here it was that the old Lady Cattermole drowned herself.

'Mother,' says the child, 'is that a dog of good family?' She is pointing to a puppy bull-dog of seven weeks old; his face is softly wrinkled. His tight velvet skin has already the delicate markings of the fullgrown brindle dog. His stomach is fat as the new-born.

Dogs in suburbs are very popular and are not trained at all not to bark. 'Why should my dog not bark if he wants to?' is rather the idea. It is a free country, they also say. But not apparently so free that you do not have to listen to the dogs barking.

Once, waking early, I heard the dog-loving woman from the next house but one talking to her friend in the street below my window. This is what she was saying:

'Seven years old 'e is.
Ever so sweet 'e is.
Ever such a neat coat 'e's got.
Ever so fond of kiddies.
But a dog likes to know oo's going to 'it 'im
    and oo isn't.'

This is the unconscious poem that happens sometimes when people are talking.

It would be wrong to suppose that everything always goes well in the suburbs. At Number 71, the wife does not speak to her husband, he is a gentle creature, retired now for many years from the Merchant Navy. He paces the upstairs rooms. His wife sits downstairs; she is a vegetarian and believes in earth currents; she keeps a middle-aged daughter in subjection. At Number 5, the children were taught to steal the milk from the doorsteps. They were clever at this, the hungry dirty children. Their father was a mild man, but the mother loved the violent lodger. When they were sent to prison for neglecting the children, the lodger bailed the mother out but let the father lie.

Life in the suburb is richer at the lower levels. At these levels the people are not selfconscious at all, they are at liberty to be as eccentric as they please, they do not know that they are eccentric. At the more expensive levels the people have bridge parties and say of their neighbours, 'They are rather suburban'.

The virtue of the suburb lies in this: it is wide open to the sky, it is linked to the city, it is linked to the country, the air blows fresh, it is a cheap place for families to live in and have children and gardens: it smells of lime trees, tar, cut grass, roses, it has clear colours that are not smudged by London soot, as are the heath at Hampstead and the graceful slopes of Primrose Hill. In the streets and gardens are the pretty trees—laburnum, monkey puzzle, mountain ash, the rose, the rhododendron, the lilac. And behind the fishnet curtains in the windows of the houses is the family life—father's chair, uproar, dogs, babies and radio.

1949

86

SIMPLY LIVING

You must have some money if you are going to live simply. It need not be much, but you must have some. Because living simply means saying No to a great many things. How can you say No to travelling up and down to work and being competitive if you do not have money? If you have a little money and are a poet, there is no greater pleasure than living simply. It is also grand. In my present circumstances I am grand. I can say No when I want to and Yes when I want to. It is important to say Yes sometimes or you will turn into an Oblomov. He stayed in bed all day and was robbed by his servants. There was little enjoyment there.

Le Plaisir aristocratique de déplaire also lies open to those who live simply. But again you must be careful, or you will cut your nose off to spite your face, and so defeat the purpose of simplicity, which is enjoyment.

> *My heart was full of softening showers,*
> *I used to swing like this for hours,*
> *I did not care for war or death,*
> *I was glad to draw my breath.*

I wrote this poem, accompanied by a drawing of a little creature swinging on his stomach on a swing, to show the enjoyment that lurks in simplicity. 'Lurks' is the word, I think. You do not seek enjoyment, it swims up to you. The writer John Cowper Powys, in his sneering, fleering humility, and from the depths of that sardonic laughter which echoes through his books and takes in the whole universe of rocks, pools, animals and human beings, knew all there is to know about the pleasures of simplicity. And its grandeurs too. For as I have hinted, there is a great lordliness in simplicity, very aggravating to bustlers, whether they bustle by choice or necessity. However, they will probably write off the simple ones, as they wrote off poor Croft:

> *Aloft,*
> *In the loft,*
> *Sits Croft;*
> *He is soft.*

I enjoy myself now living simply. I look after somebody who used to look after me. I like this. I find it more enjoyable than being looked after. And simpler. I used to have very complicated feelings about not being able to cook, supposing I ever had to, and not being able to keep house, and wondering if it might not be better being dead than not being capable. Now I cook and do not worry. I like food, I like stripping vegetables of their skins, I like to have a slim young parsnip under my knife. I like to spend a lot of time in the kitchen. Looking out into the garden where the rat has his home, and the giant hemlock is now ten feet high. (I sat next to a man at dinner the other day who during the war specialised in slow-working poisons for use by the resistance movements. He said: You want to distil the roots.) Looking at the date—1887—on my mincing machine . . . at the name 'The White Rose' on my rusty iron stove. We should thank our lucky stars for these masters of incongruity who give names . . . A Dutch blue decorated lavatory pan in a friend's house called 'The Shark'. A cruiser called Harebell. A cat, mother of 200 kittens, called 'Girlie'.

But—*Looking*. That is the major part of the simple life. Yesterday the cupboard door in my Aunt's bedroom stuck. When I wrenched it open, her father's sword fell on my head. I peeled off the perishing black American cloth it was wrapped in and looked at the beautiful sword. Its hilt was dressed in pale blue, white and gold. I looked at the blade with its beautiful chasings. *Looking at colours.* The roof-colours opposite are like the North Sea, in rain they are sapphire.

Looking at animals. The aged dog from the Dog and Duck, wobbling in fat, takes itself for walks. I met it once a mile away from home. When it crosses the road, it looks right and left like a Christian. The man in the round house collects front doors. They stand in his front garden—pink, blue, green. There is a ginger cat near us, born blind. This cat walks like an emperor, head in the air. But he is wild and if touched will fly for your throat.

Regular habits sweeten simplicity. In the middle of every morning I leave the kitchen and have a glass of sherry with Aunt. I can only say that *this is glorious*. There is a great deal of gloriousness in simplicity. There is, for instance, the gloriousness of things you only do seldom. We have not got television. But once, on a friend's set I saw 'The Trojan Women'. What laughter and argument came to me from the strong impact of this rare treat. Why make Helen out a baggage? She was royal, half-divine, and under the compulsion of a goddess. Why present the play as an argument against war, yet leave in Euripides's ironic line (which he puts in the mouth of his captive women, princesses and slaves, being led into captivity), the line: 'If we had not suffered these things we should not be remembered'. What an earth-shaking joke this is. Yet, if my life was not simple, if I looked at television all the time, I might have missed it. There are moments of despair that come sometimes, when night sets in and a white fog presses against the windows. Then our house changes its shape, rears up and becomes a place of despair. Then fear and rage run simply—and the thought of Death as a friend. This is the simplest of all thoughts, that Death must come when we call, although he is a god. It is a good thing at these moments to have a ninety-two-year-old creature sitting upstairs in her dignity and lofty intelligence, to be needed and know that she is needed. I do not think happiness in simplicity can be found in solitude, though many must seek it there, because they have no other choice . . . like this poor man I wrote a poem about and will end with:

> *Rise from your bed of languor*
> *Rise from your bed of dismay*
> *Your friends will not come tomorrow*
> *As they did not come today*
>
> *You must rely on yourself, they said,*
> *You must rely on yourself,*
> *Oh but I find this pill so bitter said the poor man*
> *As he took it from the shelf*
>
> *Crying, O sweet Death come to me*
> *Come to me for company,*
> *Sweet Death it is only you I can*
> *Constrain for company.*

Is it to avoid this *final* simplicity, that people run about so much?

1964

89